ABOUT DEREK STRINGER

Dr Derek Stringer is the radio 'voice' for Good News Broadcasting Association (UK). His broadcasts are listened to in around 180 countries each week.

Many of his messages and radio programme transcripts are available. Ask for free resources by email – info@gnba.net. Visit the website to listen to some current radio programmes – www.gnba.net

Derek travels internationally preaching at Church services, Bible Conferences and Bible Schools. You can contact him through the GNBA office.

VISIBLE GLORY
– Discover the hope of glory starting now

RESOURCES

Receive a Free Copy of Sounding Out

A free quarterly newsletter mailed by GNBA. It keeps you up-to-date with current programmes and reports on the outcome of the ministry. Devotional articles are also included.

Receive Free Transcripts

Once a month one of Derek Stringer's radio programmes or sermons is available as a free transcript to an email address as a devotional resource. Let us have your email address and you can join the worldwide family of believers taking these transcripts.

Receive a Bi-Monthly CD

By becoming a Ministry Partner with GNBA you will receive a bi-monthly CD packed with helpful Bible resources, including a message from Derek Stringer. Your financial support helps take the gospel to where radio does it best.

DEDICATION

This book is lovingly dedicated to my wife, Pauline, daughters Tracy and Clare, not forgetting my son-in-law Tony. Thank you for being the consistent encouragement that you are in the ministry the Lord has entrusted to me.

SCRIPTURES TAKEN FROM:

Authorised Version of The Bible, also known as the King James Version 1611.

The Holy Bible, New International Version

Copyright 1973, 1978, 1984 International Bible Society. Used by permission of Zondervan. All rights reserved.

The Message

Copyright 1993, 1994, 1995 by Eugene H Patterson.
Used by permission of NavPress Publishing Group.

Good News Broadcasting Association (GB)
Ranskill DN22 8NN England
Telephone: (0044) 1777817138
Email: info@gnba.net Internet: www.gnba.net

VISIBLE GLORY
-Discover the hope of glory starting now

(1) GIANTS DOWN

None of us go through life without problems and pressures. We might manage a few days or months but eventually 'something' will happen. And we'll be left asking, "What do I do now? How do I handle this giant problem in my life or in the life of someone I care about?" Problems come in all shapes and sizes.

Leo Buscaglia, in his book, BUS 9 TO PARADISE, gives a humorous picture of problems. I think you'll identify with what he wrote – *"I must confess that there are certain occurrences in my house that defy any rational explanation. For instance, one of the great and perpetual mysteries is where my socks disappear. I can't seem to keep a matching pair. I am continually having to buy new socks. After the first wash, some of them simply vanish."*

He goes on to write – "*Cartoonist Jules Feiffer expressed his puzzlement about missing socks. In his cartoon, his pathetic figure gets down to his last two pairs of socks, when his washing machine sends him a message which reads, 'Quit trifling with the laws of nature and bring me more socks.'"*

We can smile at the socks but it's harder to smile at the bigger problems.

I'm told that there are over 300 unique horrors or dislikes people talk about. That's *panics* and *dislikes* that *get out of hand in our minds and emotions.* They can push us right into insecurity and a terrible stressed-out feeling and even worse. I gather that some people even have a fear of walking into a church. Some have a fear of listening to *sermons* – that doesn't surprise me! Although I guess they may be fearing they will die of boredom! Many young people name boredom as the main reason for taking no interest in what happens beyond the church doors. For people who do get beyond those doors the battle is often with an apprehensiveness about what is about to happen – or IS happening. It can lead to the kind of trouble that can ruin our lives.

This insecurity, this lack of assurance, or downright fear – there's nothing new about it. It's an old but modern struggle. So many of us never rise up and face life with confidence because we never ever gain success or the upper-hand over the battles we have with *fear.*

Israel as a people had deep and dark fears – They feared a giant and rightly so.

**CULTIVATE AN OUTLOOK AND THE OUTLOOK IS BAD.
CULTIVATE AN UPLOOK AND THE OUTLOOK IS BETTER.**

David and Goliath is an extremely well-known and familiar story from the Bible. The children love this story don't they? The awkwardness of taking a story like this is obvious. We're inclined to say – "Let's move on to something that we *don't* know. This is kid's stuff – the *milk* of the Word and I'm ready for the *meat* – put a bit of gravy on it so that I can chew it easily – but I know this story really well. The grass has been grazed down to a bare patch!"

May I ask you to cut me some slack please? Let's see what we might just learn together from God's Word.

1 Samuel 17 is the story of David and his battle with the mighty moving mountain of a man called Goliath. This huge hippopotamus of a man. The Philistines were the big enemies of God's people Israel at that time. There were often battles between them, and the Philistines came out the winners more often than not.

On one side of the valley are the Philistines with the Israelites on the other side. Clearly neither nation wanted to take the lead and go down into the valley. That would leave them wide open to attack from their enemy.

Count Off The Strategies
Looking at this confrontation, let's take to heart some key strategies. They will help us when we need to go into a valley and meet a 'giant' of a problem – and we know it happens. Count off the strategies.

STRATEGY 1: EXPLAIN OUR GIANTS.

That is – *know* the enemy confronting us. For Israel it was obvious – it faced them across the valley on a daily basis. But it's still the starting point. Sometimes when facing a problem we can go into denial. The Israelites tried denial of a sort – difficult though, with this huge man-mountain confronting the Israelites calling for a one-to-one winner-takes-all fight. He 'mouthed off' blasphemies against the Lord. He has lots of weapons – the enemy often seems to have. That is, he had more on *his* side than they had on *theirs*. Aren't there times when we feel that way? We're so small and the enemy so big! – it's overwhelming for us. And we end up exhausted just thinking about the giant problem we must face.

Goliath gives the challenge: *"Give me a man and let us fight each other."* What Goliath is wanting to set up was usual, back in those days. One fight between a couple of soldiers and that saves all the people fighting. One representative takes the stage for them all. Should the Philistine win then Israel would have to hold their hands up in defeat. Should it be Israel that wins then the Philistines would have to do admit defeat. That's fine – just as long as you can find a willing volunteer!

God's people were "*dismayed*" and "*terrified*." These are strong words meaning *shattered* and *full of fear.* Furthermore, this *giant problem* just wasn't going to give up either. Goliath had come to bellow out his challenge against them plenty of times. Start counting twice a day for forty days and you see how often it's been! Every single morning like the *rising* of the sun – and then every night for forty days, like the *setting* of the sun – and the darkness of fear overwhelming the people because they just didn't know what to do, or where to turn.

Ever felt like that? Of course we have. Did you know that in the Scriptures forty days is many times linked to tests and trials? The question was this: Would they *run* for their lives or, would they *trust* God? This is what we find - they ran for their lives in panic.

Our Question

Here's our question -- What kind of giant are we going to have to face? What kind of giant *are* we facing? Let's clearly mark this down – this is where we have to begin.

Let me spell that out a bit more – in what *places* do we feel completely overwhelmed and thinking, "It's time to run? I just can't face any more of this pressure?" What difficulty has us held by the throat and it's choking the life out of us?

What is the *first* thing that comes to mind when we wake-up in the morning? Let me re-phrase that – what *stops* us from sleeping because it keeps going round our mind again and again and again and again?

Immediately some of us register exactly what it is. That's good! It's the starting place for handling the fear. At least we know what it is that is gnawing away at us emotionally.

Our 'Goliath' doesn't carry his weapons – *a sword and a shield* – oh no. Our giant comes at us with the weapon of *no job,* the weapon of *rejection*, the weapon of *sexual abuse,* the weapon of *chronic depression* or long-term *discouragement*, or uncertainty about our *health* or *finances* in valley circumstances. Our giant doesn't storm and parade on the hill sides of Elah like Goliath of old – oh know. He's got a weapon-like grip in our place of *work*, our *home* and whether we can keep paying the *bills*. Maybe the *exam* we must pass but can't seem to master the subject. Our giant runs to us in the shape of our *past* and the guilt that we feel about bad *choices* we've made – and we all have! Or, our giant stands and stares at us as we look onward to what the future has in store – and we don't like it one bit.

Start here

The starting point is always, in-so-far-as-we-can - **EXPLAIN OUR GIANT.** Measure it for size – *"It's more than 9 feet tall."* Call it by its name – *"This giant is Goliath* – or my *past*, my *future*, my *financial* or my *health* issues. This is my giant."

Explain what the giant is before going any further. David put it this way: "Who is this man that we should worry about him? This is a Philistine and not God's person!"

Alcoholics Anonymous has achieved a great deal for one key reason. Each member must start by naming the GIANT - *"Hello, my name is Jim, Jane, or Jerry, and I'm an alcoholic."*

This is the beginning place –It's only the start and we mustn't stop now – remember the attitude? –

CULTIVATE AN OUTLOOK AND THE OUTLOOK IS BAD.
CULTIVATE AN UPLOOK AND THE OUTLOOK IS BETTER.

STRATEGY 2: EQUIPPED FOR GIANTS.

This is where David steps on to centre stage. He had seven older brothers and he didn't count for much in the home. In fact he was often forgotten by them as he looked after the sheep.

But now he can serve a purpose for his dad Jesse. He wants news about the battle and how it's going, particularly with his older brothers. They will also need food – armies back then were often dependent upon the family.

David travels around 18 miles to bring them food. He must have left the sheep with another shepherd. I'm sure that he must have been thinking all of this through. Samuel, God's prophet picked him out for a special role in the nations - to be the king in waiting. When Samuel came calling, dad Jesse had forgotten all about David who was looking after the sheep – he needs to be reminded, "Oh yes, I do have another son". Samuel saw more than the boy and *"The Spirit of the Lord came upon David in power."*

Let's get this firmly in our minds because it's important -- David's experiences in the past **EQUIPPED** him for the current trauma. Talking to King Saul, he told him, "I've killed a lion and a bear. I can take out this Philistine."

Don't miss a key point - When facing a giant today, *look back* and see how you've been helped to handle them in your past.

God's Ways

We must keep in mind that God often works this way. We battle with some – let's say – *little* giants, although we saw them as big at the time. God saw us through – that can help us for the current really ***big*** giant.

Get the point – stick to what God has said for us to do – take care of our sheep and deal with their enemies, a lion or a bear – God's Spirit will help us there and that will get us ready to believe Him for the bigger issues.

Stick at what God wants *now* and the Spirit will help with *tomorrow*. We can better handle *tomorrow* IF we've seen how God has equipped us for our *yesterday* – do you see that? It's important.
David was chosen for his *inner* depths not his *outward* physique.

Once again, here's the attitude –

CULTIVATE AN OUTLOOK AND THE OUTLOOK IS BAD.
CULTIVATE AN UPLOOK AND THE OUTLOOK IS BETTER.

STRATEGY 3: EVADE DISCOURAGEMENTS.
David arrives on the fortieth day. He hears the giant boasting and cursing. He finds out that the king will give a lot of money tax free as well as a marriage to the winner against Goliath.

David can't listen any longer to the sarcasm of Goliath: *"Who is this man that he talks like this about our God? We have a living God don't we?"*

David's older brothers are none-to-happy about their little brother's attitude - "Look, *little* brother David – just go home to your cheeses and taking care of the *little* lambs will you. Why have you come down here? And by the way – who IS looking after the sheep with you away? We all know how full of yourself you are. You just want to come and watch the battle – that's you all over." Not that there's much of a show for David to watch at the moment is there?

Can you hear them trying to make David feel small? Eliab is a soldier and fighter and what is David? He looks after a handful of sheep. He trivialised David's job so that he can make him small. David wasn't getting any encouragement from his brothers.

Let's understand this – when knowing that we need to face up to some giant problem in our lives – there will often be the *discouragers* around us. "Oh, it's hopeless. Nothing can be done. Settle for what you've got."

Some of us know huge pressure from our family. Instead of helping they are hurting us. What they are saying doesn't build us up but breaks us down. If we are to face giants we must **EVADE DISOURAGEMENT** from whatever the source.

Negative Words
Please don't let negative words neutralise what God wants to do in our lives. Don't you think that David reacts really well? – David says: *"Now what have I done?"* How many younger brothers have said something like that! But then David says in effect – "There's good reason for me talking like this, you know!"

Always allow what we know about God to overcome what we know about the giant problem. Stop rationalising the problem. Stop blaming people or circumstance – "If they were different, life would be better!"

Frankly, David was discouraged by what his brother said but he wasn't going to let that stop him. Following David's dismissal by his brother, KING SAUL gets to hear about David's tenacious comments and wants to meet him. You get the impression that Saul is grasping at straws here.

David said to King Saul: *"Don't get disheartened by this Philistine. I will go and fight him."* Saul tries to ignore David as well – it's just his 'youth' speaking. When he grows up he'll see things differently. David says: "Look, I've killed a lion and also a bear. I've had giants of a sort in my life before, you know. I've seen what God can do." Saul says: "Okay David, it's over to you. But you'll need some armour, so put mine on." Why do you think he said that? Was he being generous? I don't think so. I think he was thinking that he would be able to redeem some credibility if David goes in his armour. If by some fluke he does win, 'I'll be able to say it's because of MY armour he did it.'

Of course it didn't fit. I guess that David's voice had an echo to it, in that huge armour. Here's a point for us - don't try fighting our giants with someone else's answers to the problem. Use the one that God is giving us.

Eliab rejects David. Saul is inclined to do the same thing. Charles Spurgeon was a great preacher from an earlier century. I like his comment on this incident: *"Many a man meets with more trouble from his friends than from his enemies."*

Just remember this:

CULTIVATE AN OUTLOOK AND THE OUTLOOK IS BAD.
CULTIVATE AN UPLOOK AND THE OUTLOOK IS BETTER.

Here's the next strategy for coping with our fears:

STRATEGY 4: EVALUATE OUR GIANTS.

In any circumstance, what we are always focuses what we see. And what we see always focuses what we do. Goliath appears to be in the family line of the giant race known as the Nephilim.

They were saying; "Goliath is so big we can't hit him." David was saying: "Goliath is so big I can't miss him! If we see ourself as a victim, that's how we'll react. But if we see ourself as a *winner* - that's how we'll react.

I remember reading about a young woman called Florence Chadwick. Back in the early 1950's, she tried swimming off the coast of California. Getting into the sea during a really heavy fog she had little idea where she was as she swam. Exhausted by the emotional strain she gave up. She then realised where she was – Just a very short distance from the finish. Later she said: "All I could see was hopeless." Her evaluation kept her from success.

Don't we all know people who say, "All I see in this problem is a fog?" If we're restrained by our apprehensiveness or feel it's no good trying - it's time to **EVALUATE** differently.

Once again –

CULTIVATE AN OUTLOOK AND THE OUTLOOK IS BAD.
CULTIVATE AN UPLOOK AND THE OUTLOOK IS BETTER.

STRATEGY 5: EMPLOY GOD'S NAME.

Goliath comes nearer to David and sees a boy. True to character he yells out: *"Am I a dog that you come at me with sticks?"* After a few 'choice' words and a mouthful of cursing he gets even more personal – *"The birds and animals are going to enjoy a good meal of you little man."*

From Backstage

Watch David right here – because David does something that none of the other men have thought of doing. He brings God from *backstage* to *centre* stage. He introduces God Almighty into the picture.

He alone was taken up with the reputation of God and His people. The others were more intent on saving their skin. David was more *'into'* affirming His God.

We have a giant-like problem in our lives – We know it and it's destroying us. My question is this - *have we brought God into the picture?* Or, *is He still waiting in the 'wings'?*

Isn't David's response just amazing - just notice the NAME he uses – it's JEHOVAH SABAOTH.
That means – "*The God of Power.*" It means, *"He is the Commander above all others."* David is probably under twenty when he says this – isn't it amazing? – *"You come against me with sword and spear and*

javelin, but I come against you in the name of the LORD Almighty, [THE COMMANDER ABOVE ALL OTHERS] *the God of the armies of Israel, whom you have defied."*

Goliath went into detail about what he would do to DAVID. Now David goes into detail about what he will do to GOLIATH. When we start to **EMPLOY** this great NAME for God and mean it – I tell you this - we will never ever see Him the same way again.

God has *unlimited* power, *unimaginable* strength and *unrestricted* ability to do what He wants as He wants and when He wants to His glory. We really can't define Him fully. We *definitely* can't deny Him anything He wants to do and when He wants to do it!

What We Know

Put all of what we know about GOD in the context of what we know about GIANT GOLIATH. God *created* the world. We meet a tall man and have to look up all the time. But put that man next to the ALPS – what happens? He becomes a dot on the horizon. If we want to *minimise* our Goliaths, then we must 'big' our God. Get the higher and bigger perspective.

We can't make God any bigger than He is already. But we *can* so focus on Him that His greatness starts to shape up our lives. *No one else* is talking about God. David talks about *no one else* but God. David sees what others are dismissing and don't want to think about. David magnifies God.

Oh yes - he sees the giant – *he's not in denial*. But – and this is important for us – David sees God more than he sees the giant. David talks of God nine times here. He talks of Goliath just a couple of times.

Focused On God

We would definitely know more spiritual victory and emotional well-being if our minds were more focused on *God* rather than our *Goliath*. For every time we focus on the giant problem – why not double or treble the times we focus on God?

Some years ago I was in Duluth in Minnesota. I got home from a meeting that I'd been speaking at. The family that I was staying with suggested I should relax, watching a Christian movie with them. I liked the music sound track. However, it was about American Football – and forgive me some of you – but that's not my passion! This is heresy to some of you – but it's not my 'game'. I do recall though how the coach, after giving himself to prayer and Bible reading got a brainwave – He said something like this - *"Our aim isn't to win games. We're here to honour God."*

If we want to cope with our apprehensions and uncertainties, our insecurities and timidity – just recall that it's God Who battles for us. The way to confront our giants is through putting our trust in God. We are not an isolated fighter. We're not all on our own.

David makes it very clear: "Our God is a LIVING God. My God isn't dead. He's not even poorly!"

Do you remember the song that was introduced to churches a few years ago - *"THE BATTLE BELONGS TO THE LORD."*

I would say this – SPEAK OUT our confidence in our God. Actually saying it out loud (if we can) will help. Confessing with our LIPS what we believe in our HEART. Say He is the Lord. Say He is MY Lord. It helps make the words real where they matter most of all, in our hearts.

EMPLOY the greatness of God into this problem not our own abilities. In David's case, the giant was an open door to know God much better. The giant problem wasn't a *barrier* in life. It was a *bridge* to experiencing God's power. If we haven't got a problem, then how do we know that God can handle it? We need problems to know that God can deal with them don't we?

At the risk of repetition but because sometimes that's a good thing –

CULTIVATE AN OUTLOOK AND THE OUTLOOK IS BAD.
CULTIVATE AN UPLOOK AND THE OUTLOOK IS BETTER.

STRATEGY 6: ENGAGE THE GIANTS.

If we get everything else right but still don't *confront* what is causing us to panic or fret – we can't win.

We must **ENGAGE** the giants, or problem, if we're going to win. David knew that he must do something about the problem immediately – no putting off the difficult moment.

David took what he was used to using with him. That was his staff and his slingshot. He then looked for five smooth stones and went off to confront this giant.

Five Smooth Stones

Why smooth stones? Because they'd move through the air much better. Why five stones? I mean – he won't get a second chance if he misses Goliath with the first stone will he? I wonder if it's because we know from elsewhere in the Bible that Goliath had four more brothers. He didn't 'get' them – some of his mighty men that surrounded him when he became King got them. But this was his confidence in the confrontation.

With this attitude David was really saying: "I'm not just after *one* giant but five!" Is it true or is it not – one with God is a majority! Don't walk or run away from a problem – face it knowing that God is with us.

Viewpoints

From David's viewpoint, God was the giant and Goliath was a little dog. Everyone else had an H. V. P. perspective. David had a D. V. P. perspective. This is the difference – HUMAN VIEW POINT against DIVINE VIEW POINT! He was so confident in this Commander God that the Bible tells us that *"He RAN quickly toward the battle line to meet him."*

If we want to be over-comers of our problems, we must take the fight to the enemy. We just can't sit back and do some wishful thinking and hope that the problem will go away.

What happened? Just a single stone from his sling and he brought down that giant. Can I risk an awful play on words? This happening was not the game-plan for Goliath. When that stone came flying in his direction – well – was this the first time that anything like that had *entered his head?* – oh dear – never mind – I apologise!

Let's get serious – how long is it since we confronted our giant? Please don't run from them. Don't build barriers against them. Don't be like Saul going into his own tent rather than facing the giant.
Will you with me take a different line of approach – a much better line of approach?

EXPLAIN the Giant – yes, he's big.

But I'm **EQUIPPED** – God has been faithful in the past and He WILL help me now.
And **EVADE** any discouragement – don't be put off by anything and anyone.
EMPLOY God's Name – He is the Sovereign Lord and in that is our security.
So – what's left to do?
ENGAGE the giant!

'Giant of STRESS - you aren't getting away with shouting at me from across the valley anymore! Giant of DEPRESSION – you want me down in the valley with you don't you – well, it's not going to happen. It may be a tough fight but you won't win against me from the valley of depression any more. Giant of ALCOHOL, Giant of PREJUDICE, Giant of SELFISHNESS -
You're going to lose you head.'

How long is it since we loaded our sling and sent a stone at our giant?

A Question
Here's a question worth thinking about -- *When did Goliath lose his life?* Is the answer when David separated his head from his shoulders? – That would do it wouldn't it? Yes – but *no*, that's not the complete answer. So, the answer has to be when that stone penetrated his skull -- is that it? Yes – but *no*, that's not the complete answer you see.

Goliath was a dead man when David *ran toward him.* That was when! Trusting God isn't saying what we believe about our giant. It's not even talking to God about it in prayer.

We may create a greater nervous tension by talking to God about it – right though that is when at the right time. You see, we can talk to God as well as to other people about the giant and make the giant even bigger in our imagination. Talk to the wrong people about a problem and they may make the problem worse. They will show you angles on the problem that you were unaware of.

I'll tell you what we need to do – Faith is making the very first step. Do you remember the old JAPANESE saying? *"A journey of a thousand miles begins with a single step"?*

If we're confused about what to do next in a crisis, this is my answer – take the very next step that you know you should take. We might not know what's round the corner after 5 or 6 steps. But we do know the next step don't we? Let's put one foot in front of the other and do what we know to do NOW!

It's time to confront our timidity and insecurity and inhibitions - CULTIVATE the UPLOOK rather than the OUTLOOK.

Start out now!

CULTIVATE AN OUTLOOK AND THE OUTLOOK IS BAD.
CULTIVATE AN UPLOOK AND THE OUTLOOK IS BETTER.

STRATEGY 7: ENVISION CHRIST.

Will you see through this great victory of David over Goliath the *greater* victory of Christ over all enemies? Goliath is called a *"Champion."* I'm told that this Hebrew word really means "A between man." Or "A mediator."

Goliath was a Philistine ambassador. God's great champion is Jesus Who was on the human side the Son of David. And Christ is our *between man.* He is our *Mediator.*

At the Cross Jesus won the fight against Satan and sin. He proved it through His *resurrection* with power and His *ascension* to the place of power. By leaving to go to the place of authority it freed up the potential of this same Christ by the power of the Holy Spirit to take up residence in us.

As we set our minds on Him and His indwelling presence do you know what it means? Yes, there are battles. Yes there are struggles. Yes there are anxious times. Yes there are uncertainties – but – setting our minds on Him leads to life and peace. It leads to a situation where *in* all things – not *outside* of them – but *in* them we can be more than conquerors.

Our Champion

Jesus is our champion. That means we're fighting battles that have already been won. Why? Because Jesus triumphed over Satan. His power is available in and through our lives.

We don't go out with five stones. We don't go against the enemy without armour. We will get into wrestling holds – but we can put on the whole armour of God. We can start to count on all that Christ has made available to us.

We don't lose heart. We can stand – and having done all – we can still stand. The apostle Peter tells us that Satan is still roaming around like a roaring lion. He tries to strike fear in us. The right Man is with us and in us. He has won the battle.

ENVISION CHRIST. He is the giant-slayer. Go down into the valley and keep in mind these seven strategies – they won't fail us - **EXPLAIN OUR GIANTS.** But don't stop there – know this – we're **EQUIPPED FOR GIANTS.** Make sure we **EVADE DISCOURAGEMENTS.** Yes – **EVALUATE OUR GIANTS.** And always **EMPLOY GOD'S NAME.** And then – **ENGAGE THE GIANTS.**

Who Are We Going To Listen To?
Don't listen to the voice of a giant. Listen to the voice of God. Acknowledge Him in all our ways. Life will be so different – we'll never want to look back with fear or look forward with foreboding.

(2) BEAUTY SEEN

A TV reporter was outlining the shocking news of the death of a young woman in an unprovoked attack. He added that the murder was even more shocking because the young woman was such an attractive person with her whole world ahead of her. In a criticism of the news report one person asked, "Would it have not been so shocking if she was unattractive and didn't have much of a future?"

I'm sure that it was an innocent remark from the young reporter but it makes you think doesn't it? However, thinking about it, we are inclined to educate children along the same lines.

The fantasy stories they hear are about beautiful princesses and charming princes. Cinderella who isn't an ugly sister. Sleeping beauty about whom the looking glass says she is the fairest in the land.

Cosmetics
Beauty is important. And we all know that cosmetics is a huge business. The word *cosmetic* has at its root *cosmos* – So it's making order out of chaos. And sometimes that's what it needs to try and do!

A mother was putting her make-up on with her young daughter watching. She asked, "Mummy what does all that paste on your face do?" "Well, darling it helps with the lines on my face." The little girl replied, "Well its working mummy because you've got a whole lot more of them now than you used to have!" *Oh dear!*

Some of the kids' jokes are cruel – "Do you think my sister is pretty?" "Well, let's just say if you pulled her pigtail she'd say, 'Oink, oink." That's not nice – but it sums up the attitude we pass on.

There's nothing new about this. In the Book of Esther there's an account of the most powerful man in the world who wants to parade his beautiful wife and she's having none of it. She's removed and the search goes out for a replacement queen. Before the contestants can meet the king they must undergo several months of beauty treatments.

A *proverb* tells us that beauty is only skin deep – but it means a lot to many people.

The famous Methodist Minister and author William Sangster shocked his London congregation when he said that he wanted to hold a beauty contest at the church. However there were conditions – all the contestants must be well over the age of forty. He was trying to get across the point that there is a big difference between *beauty* and *glamour.* Have you met elderly people of whom you have to say – "You know there's a beauty about that person." *Not glamour* – but something exudes from them that is attractive, pleasant, nice, appealing. They have a beauty of character and it shows outwardly.

The married apostle Peter wrote about how a woman shouldn't depend upon an outward show of jewellery and the like – he didn't say she shouldn't use it – but he wanted an unfading beauty of a gentle and quiet spirit.

A German Theologian of another generation by the name of Helmut Thieleke has put it like this it – '*The lines of LAUGHTER around the eyes are as much a sign of godliness as much else we think passes off as it.'*

I think he was right! I recall listening to a missionary back in England from South America. He spoke about preaching from the *para-message.* That is – we say something but what we are is also speaking. And sometimes people are listening more to what we are than to what we say.

When the *para-message* is attractive it adds a magnetic quality to the words we use. And people are drawn to the truth we communicate. Again I think he was right.

Let's find out from God's Word what it has to say about *beautiful lives.*

1) MAKE SPIRITUAL BEAUTY OUR AIM.

There is a beauty that we should really want. The Psalmist knew this when in Psalm 90:17 he made this his prayer: "May the *favour* of the Lord our God rest upon us." The word for *favour* can be translated *beauty*. That's the word in the King James Version of the Bible.

We pray for many things both for ourselves as well as the people that we care about. How often do I pray for the beauty of the Lord to show through me? A sense of His favour, approval, grace or esteem.

How often does it enter my mind and heart that this is something that He wants me to really want?

Why should we make this our aim?

The Purpose of God

One reason is – because it's the PURPOSE of God. Psalm 149:17 puts it like this: "The Lord takes delight in His people; He *crowns* the humble with salvation." The word *crowns* has the idea of *beautifying*. Royalty wear a crown – it sets them apart. They belong to a special group. God wants us to know that we reign with Him and are seen outwardly to belong to Him.

God's intentions are that we should be marked out by sheer beauty of character. It should make us stand out in a crowd. Don't you think that at times we have too narrow a view of Christianity? We think in terms of what we believe – is it an orthodox belief? We can so easily forget Christlikeness of life. We think in terms of lots of people coming to church and a busy programme of events. Increased giving, a flow of conversions.

All these are good and within the scope of what God wants. But my question is this: How often do we pray for beauty of character? How often do we make it our prayer that people will see us crowned – clearly set apart as under God's favour – not because we tell them that, but because they see it?

'Let the favour *(or beauty)* of our God be upon us.' This is something I should want. It's God's PURPOSE for us.

The Person of God

We also find this in God's PERSON – Our Lord Jesus Christ. The prayer is for the favour or beauty of OUR LORD to be upon us.

There's an old song some of you may recall:
"Let the *beauty* of Jesus be seen in me."

It's interesting that we will make that our song and prayer but Isaiah predicted that when Christ came He would have no beauty or majesty to attract people. You see, it wasn't outward show. There is a beauty of character in Jesus, and with Jesus living in us surely that will make a difference.

There's a story told of a little girl walking out of church after a Sunday morning service. She said to her mother that the sermon confused her. Asked in what way, this was her reply – "The pastor said that Jesus is bigger than us." "Yes that's right." "He also said that Jesus lives in us. Well, if He's bigger than us and lives *in* us, won't he show *through* us?"

More often than not, God isn't wanting to teach us anything new. He is wanting us to *show* what we *know*! Our lives revealing the radiant attractiveness of Christ. This should be our AIM. But we need to note this can be our SHAME.
That's the second point we need to note.

2) NO SPIRITUAL BEAUTY OUR SHAME.

The beauty God wants us to AIM at can be missed completely. The city of Jerusalem was given a great title – *the perfection of beauty.* What a great description! But a day came when God's prophets thundered out concerning this city, *"All her beauty is gone!" The shame of it.*

Why can we lose what God wants us to have, and in our better moments we want too? One reason is because God takes it away! We're being disciplined.

Two verses in our Bible tell us that God's discipline acts like that of a *moth*. Psalm 39:11, *"You rebuke and discipline men for their sin; you consume their wealth like a moth."* Hosea 5:12, God says: *"I am like a moth to Ephraim."*

I know something about moths. I've gone to a cupboard to take clothes out and found there's been a silent *eater* at work! There are times when God acts like a moth! Silently and secretly He lets the decay happen to our Christian lives. And it's because we don't take care to know something better. God says, "Very well, you won't learn the easy way; I'll teach you a harder way."

Israel had forgotten God. She had compromised herself. So, God disciplined her and withheld blessings with the hope that she would learn and seek His face. It's the same for us.

It's not an easy question for us to ask ourselves but it's a necessary one – is there a disappearing beauty? Are we becoming more Christ-like, or less?

When there's something wrong in us, we're in danger of presuming that because we're Christian, with knowledge of God's Word, perhaps looked up to by people around us – we can pick and choose what we are before God. Do you know what God says: "The beauty and favour that you once had will develop flaws. Originally you were mine, but now I'll be like a *moth."*

Who wants to be a *moth-eaten* Christian? It can happen. *Beauty* can be lost because it's taken away – or, it may be because we take ourselves away from where it can be found.

We start thinking that beauty can be found where there is none. What we think is attractive is a mirage of temptation.

We live in a day when sin is glamorised. Our celebrity culture makes a lot out of the *'beautiful people'.* But much of this is a deception. It will take us away from God and His best for our lives.

It's so important to see what just a 'skin deep' beauty is. Outwardly attractive but no depth to it. It's a temptation that takes us away from God.

There's a beauty that must be our AIM. A beauty that can be SHAMED – we can lose it or spoil it. But there's a beauty that can be RECLAIMED.

3) SPIRITUAL BEAUTY RECLAIMED.

It comes as we aim at HOLINESS. Psalm 96:9 spells it out: "Worship the Lord in the splendour *(or beauty)* of His holiness."

Holiness?

What is Holiness? The root meaning of *holiness* in the Old Testament is separateness, or separation. Separation from what? From everything that's out of sync with what God wants. Separateness from sin. That's the kind of beauty that God offers to us, and which God says can be found. This is the beauty or splendour of holiness – separateness from sin; and apart from that there is no beauty or splendour about us.

The Opposite
Just think about the opposite of holiness – it's not beautiful. Can we describe people as having a *beautiful temper?* What a *beautiful gossiper* they are! And have you noticed how *beautifully unkind* that person is! How *beautifully touchy* they are! How *beautifully offended* they become and so easily! How *beautifully jealous,* isn't it lovely! How *beautifully unfaithful!*

These things are made to look good at the movies but they're ugly in our homes. ALL sin is ugly even when it's painted in bright colours. The devil may try to deceive us into thinking it doesn't really matter – but there's a price to pay. The only beauty and splendour that God offers is the beauty of holiness.

The Bible speaks of the beauty of holiness as separateness from sin. Don't you think that one of the greatest needs in our churches today is to be prepared to call sin what it is – *sin.*

Have you ever wondered what John was meaning when he wrote, *"If we claim we have not sinned, we make Him out to be a liar and His Word has no place in our lives."* He is writing to Christians and most wouldn't claim that they've not sinned! But we do go down the road of not calling sin what it is – sin! When we don't get on with someone - we don't call it sin, we call it an incompatibility of temperament problem.

For the beauty and the splendour of our Lord to display from us – we must face up to holiness and what it means for us.

But where is it found? We want to RECLAIM it – where do we go to get it? Psalm 27:4 gives us the answer: *"One thing I ask of the Lord, this is what I seek: that I may dwell in the house of the Lord all the days of my life, to gaze upon the beauty of the Lord and to seek Him in His temple."*

As we focus on Him in worship, in His Word, in thanksgiving – something will start to happen. As the New Testament puts it – we're transfigured, or changed, by the Spirit of the Lord in ever-increasing splendour into His own image.
This beauty that is to be our AIM can be SHAMED – when we lose it. But it can be RECLAIMED – and it can REMAIN! It will be a visible evidence of our involvement with God. Remember what they said of the early disciples – they took note that they had been with Jesus.

What Is Noticed

Do people notice that about us? Visit some countries – particularly in Africa – and believers are so keen. They will introduce themselves and immediately give you their testimony. They have a sheer joy in telling you about what Christ means to them. Wonderful though that is – it's occurred to me that the early Christians didn't *give* a testimony first of all. They were *called* Christians! It's good to *give* a testimony from our lips – and don't get this wrong – I'm not criticising that for one moment. But isn't it something very special when people simply note that there's something of Christ about us and we haven't had to say anything? There's something distinctive, something that demands an explanation in terms of God!

When His beauty shines out it will attract interest. Probably unconsciously so. Remember how it did that for Moses? He had been in the presence of God and had no idea that his face was shining with the glory of it all. There will be a shining out of the living Christ through us. People will be drawn to *Christ* not us, but *through* us.

Challenge of the Gospels

Have you noticed the challenge from the ministry of Jesus in the Gospels? We read, "They came to Him." He was not running after them. He didn't invite them to come. They came! What a contrast with the average Christian don't you think? How many people are drawn to Christ through us?

Maybe our home or place of work is indifferent to the claims of Christ. Maybe we have a rough time there. Maybe we've been praying that it will change. Keep praying – but we need more than that! More than anything else it's the quality of our life – it's the beauty of our character that we reveal that counts. It's no good saying "I'm a Christian" if He can't be seen in me.

Beauty on Us

May the *beauty* of the Lord our God be upon us. Worship Him. Stay focused on Him. Keep thanking Him for who He is and what He is doing and will do. Keep walking with Him. His presence will rub off on us. What a difference it will make. Gaze upon the beauty of the Lord and seek Him. Make it the one thing we ask. The one thing we seek.

(3) WALLS UP

In his book *Straight Talk to Men and Their Wives,* Dr James Dobson tells a story about a 10-year-old boy. His name was Robert. His parents were friends of the medical doctor who noticed Robert needed a dentist. He was a really obnoxious boy and the staff hated it when they saw he had an appointment with them. The doctor selected an older experienced dentist. It led to a fascinating encounter. Let me use some of Dr Dobson's words in telling you what happened next.

Robert arrived but wouldn't get in the dentist chair. He said, "If you make me get in that chair, I will take off all my clothes." The dentist calmly said, "Son, take 'em off." The boy did in his defiance. "All right, son," said the dentist, "Now get in the chair." Robert did as he was told. When instructed to step down from the chair he demanded his clothes back. The dentist said he could pick them up tomorrow. Later his mother contacted the dentist to thank him.

This is what she said – *"You don't know how much I appreciate what happened yesterday. You see, Robert has been blackmailing me about clothes for years . . . YOU ARE THE FIRST PERSON TO CALL HIS BLUFF, doctor, and the impact on Robert has been incredible."*

I don't know how parents today would react to this or how right the approach was – dubious, I think. However, Nehemiah would have cheered the man on because he knew how to handle messy situations and deal with them for the best. Don't we want to take awkward situations and mend them?

It Happens!

Have you ever noticed that once we start to want to do things God's way and serve His purposes, things can get very messy? Peter the apostle knew the truth of this didn't he? – he put it this way: *"Do not be surprised at the painful trial you are suffering, as though something strange were happening to you."*

I meet people who are surprised and often thrown into turmoil when life doesn't retain a well-ordered line. We can make a big choice when this happens to us and life falls into disarray. We can *give up* on God, or we can *give in* to God. I want to propose with Nehemiah in mind that we face a crisis with confidence.

Back Home

Let's take a look at what happens in NEHEMIAH Chapter 4. The people have returned from exile and they're back in their own land. They're trying to work hard and get the walls of the old city of Jerusalem up and secure all over again – a massive task for a fairly small work-force. The *"People worked with all their heart."* And then low spirits, a loss of morale and pessimism takes charge of all the people.

"When Sanballat heard that we were rebuilding the wall, he became angry and was greatly incensed. He ridiculed the Jews . . . What are those feeble Jews doing?"

Notice that he called these workers "feeble" – that's – *pathetic, grim faced, losers!* You know, whenever we try getting involved in God's work we will always have to face opposition.

Our motto must be –

**FACING A CRISIS,
FACE IT WITH CONFIDENCE!**

Are we dismayed by life's circumstances today? Do we feel like giving up? Nehemiah 4 reveals three reasons for it back then – and I don't think that you'll spot any difference as the years have ticked by.

CAUSE FOR GIVING UP NUMBER 1: WEARY.

They are battling with overtiredness. "The people in Judah said, 'The strength of the labourers is *giving out.*'" In straightforward language – these workers were exhausted. They were going full pelt and needed a break. The words, *"giving out"* have the idea of "stumbling around." Has that ever happened to you? You just can't seem to put one foot in front of another – we've all known that. A good night's sleep will often be enough. But at some times that doesn't work.

When we're *physically drained of energy,* it's so easy to want to give up and go and bury our head in the sand. It just takes one more problem – however small – to do it.

It's right that we also notice something fascinating here – look at *when* the people became tired-out and despondent. It was when the building was *half* built. Going up but not yet completed.

I've often noticed this – we start new projects, and what happens? The first half goes really fast, we're full of enthusiasm and we wonder where the time went. We're enthusiastic to get the job done. But, after a while the enthusiasm of something new wears thin. The work becomes 'business-as-usual' and just a duty. It's then that we can end up feeling listless and lethargic.

So, what did the people say to Nehemiah? "We can't rebuild the wall." Yes – It's just too much for us. These are just the same people who were working with all their energy to get the project done. What has happened?

They are WEARY. And that brings us to the second reason as to why they want to give up rather than go on –

CAUSE FOR GIVING UP NUMBER 2: WARY.

There is so much chaos. It's like a bomb has hit the site – It's looks nuclear! So many obstacles in the way, it's made them unsure of themselves and inclined to exasperation.

A Scenario

What do you think of this scenario? We want to serve our Lord. We don't want to just *'polish a seat'* in church. We want to be and do something. But look at the chaos and the people I'm meant to work with! Be careful here, because they are also looking at *me!*

Isn't it true though that we can be left with the feeling – *This is just too much. The task is too big. We can't achieve something for God and his cause.* A lot of people who go to church function this way.

WEARINESS in service. WARINESS at achieving anything through what we do. But there's even more cause for our dismay.

CAUSE FOR GIVING UP NUMBER 3: WORRY.

The enemies of the Lord's work had caused them to worry about their own safety and they felt like running for cover. Notice who is getting the most worried and stressed - "Then the Jews *who lived near them* came and told us ten times over 'Wherever you turn, they will attack us.'" Those people most impacted by the worry were the people living the nearest to the enemies.

Thinking it Through
Do we struggle with worry and anxiety a lot? Do we try to contain it but can't? Somehow it seems to break free and start to choke us?

This isn't the complete answer but it goes some way to help – to handle worries and anxieties - watch the people we mix and mingle with. If we stay close to people *smelling* of worry, just like cigarette smoke, it will hang around us too! It will get on our clothes and in our lungs.

If WEARINESS, WARINESS and WORRY are some of the REASONS for our dismay, what are some REMEDIES? Don't we want to say 'good-bye' to discouragement in our service for God. If we understand the way that it was handled in Nehemiah's day we'll have the answer. We'll be able to go from this message into whatever mess and keep serving the Lord.

REMEDY 1: CONSULT GOD.

That seems a simple thing to observe but it's essential and we mustn't move too quickly over it - Nehemiah looked up before looking around. He prayed and opened his heart to God.

The Principle
Isn't this amazing? Here's the principle we learn from Nehemiah. When there's *negative* talk all around us the most *positive* thing is to talk to God. Don't join the negative discussion – CONSULT GOD.

They *prayed* to God and *posted* a guard. When their enemies started talking, Nehemiah kept on praying and the people stayed balanced.

REMEDY 2: CHECK PRIORITIES.

Any enemies about to attack would probably do it at their most vulnerable points. So Nehemiah put special guards at these locations.

Question
Where are we most vulnerable?

Do we have a weak marriage? Please don't too easily walk away from it. Let's try changing our way of handling the broken down walls and accusative barbed comments. Get some help if we can. Make it a priority to do something with it.

Is there disarray in our job? Don't think it's got to be the end! Change our priorities.
Are we bringing God into our place of work through our attitudes?

Don't stop living for the Lord Jesus! Yes – life is busy but schedule time with Him. It's really important. Make it a regular meeting. Get connected to a small group at our church if we can. Don't let discouragement overwhelm and exhaust us. Take action wherever we can.

REMEDY 3: CONTEMPLATE GOD.

Nehemiah looked at everything – the broken down walls, the enemies, the disheartened people and Nehemiah motivates his people.

"Don't be afraid of them. Remember the Lord, who is great and awesome."

They needed to contemplate the kind of God they had and what He had said to them. The people grumbled about all the mess. Here's a question. Wasn't that chaotic mess there when they first arrived? Of course it was. What is the difference now? They had been focused on God, what He was like and what He would do – but now they've taken their eyes off God and on to the mess!

Make a Decision
Let's decide to be '*lookers*' at GOD rather than '*lookers*' at the MESS – Good idea? We can change our broken messed up world – but – just like Nehemiah there are certain attitudes that are essential.

Actually, if we take the word CHANGE – C. H. A. N. G. E. – it may help us to mark down what these attitudes are.

C-ONSIDER God's Word.

In Nehemiah 8, Ezra started reading at the beginning of the day until lunchtime. All the people listened to God's Word for over six hours! This went on for a full week. And, they didn't just sit in nice comfortable church seats – They "listened attentively." Do you know that there's nothing more warming for a preacher than when people listen attentively to God's Word and really do *consider* what it's personally saying to them.

I want to learn from Ezra's example therefore, I'm going to start a campaign to have 6-hour long Church Services! What do you think? That's not true – honest! But when Ezra opened the book the people respected God by standing up. That still happens in some churches and denominations – This is where it goes back to. You see, they knew this wasn't just an ordinary human being speaking to them – no - they were hearing what their great and powerful and awesome God was saying to them.

After Ezra praised "The great God". Do you see what the people did? All the people lifted their hands and responded, "Amen! Amen!" No one fell asleep in this service did they? Everyone really *considered* carefully and wanted to be *doers* of the Word. Following this, they *"Bowed down and worshipped the Lord with their faces to the ground."*

Connecting With God

Hearing God through His Word in this way meant that they were completely taken up by it. They were connecting. They were *'in the zone'*, targeted and even more willing to hear from their great God.

The Levites join Ezra in helping to instruct and teach the people. They *"made it clear"* and gave the sense of what was being heard - *"so that the people could understand what was being read."* They probably mixed in with groups of the people, walking around and helping to explain and answer questions. Probably some kind of Q and A. There was a public reading of God's Word in a large crowd and then face-to-face talk-back times in small groups.

That's because the Bible is divinely inspired and designed to be understood. You and I need to contemplate the Word privately, hear it preached corporately, and then apply it in a small-group community.

So they changed for the better in the middle of the mess because they CONSIDERED GOD'S WORD.

H-ELPING One Another.

Nehemiah 3 shows how people who work with one another will achieve so much more than if just one person tries to do all the work. We are all to be involved because we're important. Think how Paul put it when he pictured the church as a *body*. Some parts are more obvious than others but all are important in playing their part for the good of the whole.

We can't do everything. But we can do something. We are saved to function by HELPING one another. Do you realise that not one church has just one pastor or minister? Every church should have as many pastors and ministers as it has people attending a Sunday morning service! Christianity isn't for spectators but participators.

What Nehemiah tried to do was this – he worked his HELPERS together. *"We're not just doing this for ourselves. This is for God and His glory."*

Sometimes we think too individualistically about our faith. Remember the family prayer that Jesus taught? Our Father – give us. Not *my* but *our*. And not give *me* but *us!* There is a corporate dimension to our faith so that we support and supplement one another.

This brings me to the next thing we need to note if we are to change in the middle of a mess that's so disheartening –

C-ONSIDER God's Word.
H-ELP one another.

A-SK of God.

We make changes this way. Do you know that there are twelve different prayers in Nehemiah? They are prayers of *despair*, *delight*, *dependence* and *dedication*.

Are we determined to ASK OF GOD? It's been well said that - *prayer isn't getting what we wish for done in heaven. It's getting what God wishes for done on earth.*

Mending a mess comes as we ASK the God who can make order out of chaos. He can do that in us and for us. Maybe we have not because we just don't ask. Or, maybe we ask but it's such a general prayer – we will never know if the answer has been given!

NURTURE Our Worship.

Worship has been defined as "WORTH-SHIP" – We see God as WORTH IT so we WORSHIP! Nothing else that we humans do comes anywhere close NURTURING worship in ourselves and with one another.

Turning to Nehemiah 12:27, we read about a special Service of DEDICATION for the newly built city wall. When the Levites came together they met *"To celebrate joyfully the dedication with songs of thanksgiving and with the music of cymbals, harps and lyres."*

This is going to sound so ordinary you may wonder why I bother to write it – but it's necessary – for me at least! Worship is all about God not about me! It's not ultimately a question of musical taste but of content.

Praise has to be a priority over our likes and dislikes. Have you noticed it's much easier to start getting selfish when we start singing? The aim of our praising is to centre on God and assist the people around us to do the same. The secret of acceptable worship isn't *what* we do but the *way* we do it. The new residents of the city of Jerusalem had hearts full of joy as well as songs of praise and thanks.

Worship was never meant to be a colourless boring thing. There was nothing limited about the style of their thanksgiving service. A wide and varied selection of musical gifts were used to NURTURE the worship of the people. There's nothing lethargic about their joyful praise because it spills out from people grateful to have personally experienced the amazing goodness and grace of God.

Nehemiah 9:4 describes another kind of worship time. The Levites form two groups. Some standing on the stairs on one side of the crowd. The other group stood across from them. These two groups called out across the people - one group was confessing the people's sins. The other was praising God for His greatness.

Group One "called with loud voices." This meant they *yelled out!* Group Two concentrated on singing about God's character.

The rest of the chapter is about their guilt, followed by praise shouts all about God's amazing power and willingness to stay involved with them. There are tears of *grief* and tears of *joy*.

Do you see that, if this is in any way a template for our worship services today, they should be identified with two things - *REVERENCE* and *REJOICING*. The great need of the church in our day is a refreshed understanding of God's presence with us.

Notice that the worshippers invite all the people to, *"Stand up and praise the Lord your God, who is from everlasting to everlasting. Blessed be your glorious name, and may it be exalted above all blessing and praise."*

God's people meditate on God's personality and power as displayed through His mighty works in history. If we're fumbling around with our faith today - it may well be because our perspective of God is too small or too limited.

Theologian David Wells calls this: *"The weightlessness of God."* He writes that our sense of weakness or feebleness can be tracked to our limited appreciation and experience of the kind of God we have. This is how he put it: *"GOD rests too inconsequentially upon the church. His truth is too distant, His grace too ordinary, His judgment too benign, His gospel too easy, and His Christ too common."*

Changed Through Worship
Worship should change the way we live. If worshippers leave a service with no thought of becoming more like God in their lives, then the aim of worship hasn't been fulfilled. If people continue to be selfish, proud, arrogant, critical, or immoral, then there's been a breakdown somewhere in what should be happening to change us for the better – despite the mess around us.

CHANGE comes as we –
C-ONSIDER God's Word.
H-ELP One Another.
A-SK God.
N-URTURE Worship.
And the next thing –
G-UARDIANSHIP For One Another.

Reading through Nehemiah we can't help notice the community starts to push the self-destruct button because of some festering hurts. The workers now face another enemy much more tricky to handle than the enemy outside of them as a people. And the timing of the problem couldn't have been more a problem. "The walls are now built - but here comes another fine mess you've got me into!" That's what Nehemiah may have been thinking.

Coming to the fifth chapter, Nehemiah has to turn his attention from the building project to the builders themselves! The enemies outside had a way of making them guardians of one another. They were looking out for one another – But all this *internal* conflict threatened to divide and ruin them. It's much easier to conquer an enemy who attacks us from the outside than it is to forgive a friend who hurts us. In the midst of a great work for a great God - the people start making a lot of noise against their own Jewish brothers – their family!

This wasn't just a little upset or a small problem. Nehemiah stops all that he's doing to tackle the division. Why? Because God's people must guard their relationships with one another. He appeals to their love. He reminds them of God's great and good purposes. And he tries to inspire them to remember their witness to others around them.

There's a direct connection between the effectiveness of our work for the Lord and how we connect with one another. If we're in conflict right now with someone, take the action necessary, meet and make it right. Get the help of someone else if necessary – After all, the people needed Nehemiah's help.

Guardianship over our relationships is absolutely vital to *change* for the better. This leaves us with one more point –

E-VANGELISE People.

Nehemiah 12:31 shows the action that they took. The leaders went up on the top of the wall. Remember what their enemies had said? *"Those walls are so weak that a fox could knock them down."* What's happening now? Here the people are marching on top of the walls!

It was a wonderful opportunity to prove the point that *"This work had been done with the help of our God."* As they marched on top of the walls everyone could see what was happening. All around the city people could look and hear the people's praise. *"The sound of rejoicing in Jerusalem could be heard far away."*

Is God creating within us a massive and huge desire to tell the *outsiders* so that they can become *insiders* and know not just about Jesus through our songs - but by being part of it?

I remember a man from the building trade. He had his own business and it was a success. He used to come to church service often and never sang. He was always respectful and liked listening to other people sing but he felt he would be a hypocrite if he joined in. One day he saw that his life was not in sync with God. He saw what Jesus had done just for him at the Cross. He owned up to the mess and confessed Christ. It was *then* that he sang – and the rest of us were struggling to do so because of the emotion of the moment. Later he would tell me that the songs of the people had been a witness to him. That's how it can be.

Let's come back to our motto for today – Remember! –

FACING A CRISIS,
FACE IT WITH CONFIDENCE!

God will build from the mess when we let Him change things His way.

This is it and it works for C. H. A. N. G. E. – **CHANGE** -
CONSIDER God's Word.
HELP One Another.
ASK God.
NURTURE Worship
GUARDIANSHIP For One Another.
EVANGELISE Others.

But first we must make sure Christ is in our lives so that He can be the *change agent* from the inside out. It's time to come to Him.

In one of his books, Max Lucado writes a moving account about a young Brazilian girl. She had hopes and desires to see the world. Her home was poor. She slept on the floor. She fantasised about a life in the city which would be so much better than this. One morning she quietly left home with her mother distraught. She knew what life on the city streets would be like for her young and attractive daughter. Maria quickly got a few things together and went out to find her daughter. On her way to the bus stop she sat in the photo booth spending all she could on pictures of herself. With her collection of small photos, she got on the bus for the city. Maria knew Christina wouldn't be able to earn money and that she was far too stubborn to admit failure. When hungry and in need - a person will do things that were before never in their mind.

So, Maria started searching for her daughter in bars, nightclubs and hotels. Wherever she looked she left her own photo—stuck on a bathroom mirror, taped to a hotel bulletin board, pinned to a telephone booth. And on the back of the picture she wrote a short note for Christina. It wasn't long before both her money and the photos were all gone. Maria was forced to go home. The exhausted mother cried as the bus began its long journey back home to her little village. Just a few weeks later, Christina came down the hotel stairs. She was looking older than her years. Her light laugh was gone. Her dream had turned into a nightmare. Many times she'd just longed to trade these sordid hotel rooms for her own home. Yet the village was another life and far too distant. Reaching the bottom of the stairs, she noticed the face of her own mother in a photo. Christina froze. Then took hold of the small picture. Written on the back were these words –

"WHATEVER YOU HAVE DONE,
WHATEVER YOU HAVE BECOME,
IT DOESN'T MATTER.
PLEASE COME HOME."

She did.

It's Time

God gave us today and it's time to let Him mend the mess of our lives. To take the chaos and create what only He can do. Acknowledge Him and let Him take us and use us, to build our lives for time and eternity – a building that will never collapse.

A life that outlasts times itself. *It's time!*

(4) AN EVENING AND MORNING MEAL

When Jesus had a meal with people it did more than feed their body. A lot can happen around a meal when it involves Jesus. This chapter will check out two meals – one was in the evening and the other was early morning. The first was before the Cross (John 13). The other was after His resurrection (John 21).

A mother wanted to help her little children understand the meaning of Easter in a creative way, so she decided to re-enact the Last Supper. She made a dinner of lamb, because that's what Jesus and his disciples would have eaten. She took a table to the upstairs bedroom because the Last Supper was eaten in an upper room. She spent all day on this. But before they could even say grace, her children got in a fight over who was going to get to sit in their favourite chair. The evening ended with her kids yelling at her, "You are the meanest Mummy ever." Don't you just love it when children say that to you? It's like they have this special award ceremony: "*The Meanest Mummy Ever* Oscar goes to ..." Well she was discouraged about all of that until she remembered that that's actually how the real Last Supper went down.

Four days before the real Last Supper, Jesus had marched into Jerusalem on Palm Sunday and the crowds went crazy thinking He was going to kick out the Romans. So in response to that, the disciples started to jockey for power and position. Who's going to be Vice Messiah?

By the time they got to the Last Supper they didn't want to serve anyone. All they wanted was to get power and position, so they got in a big fight. Do you know what over? Their favourite chair! Who was going to get to sit in the seat of honour. So, you see, that mother's children weren't misbehaving. They were simply imitating the disciples. What more could a mother ask for?

A Shock

Nobody wanted to serve anybody else. They were just in it for what they could get for themselves. In the middle of all of this arguing over power and position Jesus does a shocking thing. He washes his disciples' feet. He serves them. It's actually a living parable of who Jesus is.

In this story, Jesus lays aside his garments just as he had to lay aside the comforts of heaven to come to earth. He puts on a towel, just like as God He wraps himself in human flesh. He washes their feet to make them clean just as He died to cleanse us from our sins. Then He stood back up and went to His seat just as He was raised from the dead. It is a living parable about a God who serves and who loves. It was also a very scandalous thing to do. Because back in Jesus' day with all that walking around on dusty roads in leather sandals, feet had some interesting odours, and washing them was considered so disgusting that not even a slave had to do it. But here Jesus, God in human form, washes His disciples' feet. It is a model of serving others.

Truth be told, it is a model that we don't much want to follow. Honestly speaking, the whole idea of serving others doesn't always excite us. Very few of us get up every morning and think, "How can I serve someone else," or, "My, I hope someone cuts me off in traffic today, so I can serve them by letting them have my place." Very few of us do that. If we're honest, serving others is something we think of as a "have to do" or an "ought to do," not a "get to do." Sometimes that's how we preachers make it sound.

One man told me that when he was a child his younger brother would never be able to get to sleep unless the dog slept in the bed right beside him. So every night he would call, "Here, here, let's go to bed." And the dog would run away. So his brother would hunt her down and grab her by the front paws and drag her down the hall to his bedroom, which didn't hurt the dog, but her back feet would be frantically pawing trying to get away, and she'd be growling and snarling the whole way down the hall. The dog did not want to serve his brother.

Sometimes I think that's how we respond to Jesus' call to go serve: we kind of growl and snarl all the way. But I think this story of Jesus washing his disciples' feet gives us two reasons that we can serve not out of guilt, not out of duty, not out of obligation: we can serve in joy.

1) SERVE IN JOY BECAUSE WE HAVE BEEN SERVED.

Preachers usually use this as a story about how we ought to go out and serve others, and it is that. But it is first a story about how much we have been served. It's a story about a God who loves us enough to wash our feet. And when we really understand that, not just in our heads but in our hearts, it makes it easier to go out and serve others in joy. When we realise everything that God has done for us, when we really get that in our hearts it gives us a little bit more motivation to serve others. And God has done a lot. The biggest thing God has done for us is He loves us even when we are unlovable.

This story of foot washing is a good metaphor for that. Feet are weird, feet are dirty, and feet smell funny. Weird, messy, smelly: that's me! And I think that describes a lot of us in some ways. We've all got junk. We all have our sins. Jesus knows all that. He sees all the dark and ugly thoughts we think. He sees what we do when we're alone and think no one's looking. He sees all of that but He still loved us enough to die for us anyway, which must mean that we are very valuable.

Good Gifts

He's blessed us with good gifts like friends and families, the opportunities we've had in life. When we really get in our hearts how much He has given us, it becomes a lot easier to give ourselves away and serve others.

It's the rhubarb principle. We used to have a small patch in our garden which just grew and grew. I love the stuff but we'd start giving it away. "Have some rhubarb." Because we're awash in the stuff. Here's the deal: we live in a world that tries to convince us, mostly through advertising, that we don't have enough. We don't have enough stuff, we don't have enough love, and we don't have enough whatever it is. But if we take time to really experience how much God has given us, we realise our hands are filled with blessings. When we really understand that, it becomes a lot easier to give ourselves away, and serve in His name.

How can we do that? How can we experience God's love and God's blessing in such a way that we will be motivated to give? Here are three suggestions.

One: Let Jesus In.

In this story Peter proudly says, "Lord, you don't need to wash my feet. I've got clean feet. Wash the other guys' feet. Take a whiff, they need it. But not me, Lord." That's sometimes how I think we are with Jesus: we don't want to let Him in. We don't want Him to see our junk, or admit that we have it. But when we let Jesus in and start being honest about those lustful thoughts, or our anger issue, or the terrible things we think about other people, when we get honest with Jesus and admit those things, then we can really begin to experience Jesus saying to us: “I love you. This does not define you. I forgive you. I can help you overcome this.” We need to let Him in, daily.

Two: Let Other People Care for Us.
I think that’s pretty hard to do. In fact, as hard as it is to go and serve others, I think it is sometimes even harder to let others serve us, isn’t it? We are a proud, “I’ll do it myself” kind of people. Being served makes us feel needy. We don’t like that.

A Pastor has written: ‘A while back I was leading a men’s Bible study. One night we were studying about washing feet. Suddenly one of the guys said, “Hey, I’ve got a great idea. I’ll go get a bowl full of water, and the Pastor here can wash all of our feet. He’s the pastor. And then we’ll wash his.”’ He said, “I was like, whoa, whoa, whoa. Who said we were actually going to do what’s in the Bible? This is merely theoretical, you understand. The mere thought of that - sort of just gave us this collective sense of the willies. It seemed too vulnerable and weird.”

He added: “But what I realised in that moment was, given the choice, I would rather wash someone’s feet than have someone wash my feet. I don’t want to be cared for. I don’t want to be served. Besides, I have a weird looking toe and I didn’t want anyone to see it. But when we let people in, when we let them care for us, listen to us when we have a problem, help us when we have a need, we’re letting them be Jesus with skin on, and we can experience Jesus loving us through them.”

Three: Reflect On Jesus’ Love.
Prayer, meditation, Scripture. Think about the Cross and say this over and over to yourself: He did that for me. He did that for me. He wore the chains so I could be free. He did that for me. When we experience how much God loves us, by letting Him in, by letting others serve us, by reflecting on His love, when we know how much we have been served, then we can serve in joy.

2) SERVE IN JOY IS BECAUSE OF PROMISED BLESSING.

I am one of those people who don’t always feel like serving. But one of the things that motivates me to serve is I trust Jesus’ promise that if I serve there will be a blessing, I will know Him more, I will have joy as I do it. I have served based on that promise, and what I've discovered is, Jesus is always right. Even when it's hard, serving gives us joy. There are lots of ways to serve, and when we do, we have joy.

How will you put yourself in a position to experience God's radical love for you? And how can you find the joy He promises that comes from giving that love away, and serving others in His name?

We have been talking about significant moments in Jesus' ministry that happen around meals. As you know, the first meal recorded in the Bible was when Adam and Eve ate the forbidden fruit, and as a result of that, sin, death, suffering, insecurity, all kinds of things entered into our world, and we started to see God not as a loving father but as a cruel tyrant out to blast us if we did anything wrong. But at the Last Supper God reverses that image of Himself. God Himself in human form takes up a basin and a towel to wash His sinful disciples' feet, even Peter's feet, who is going to deny Him, He even washed Judas' feet, showing once and for all that He is not a cruel tyrant, He is a loving father who came not to judge us, not to lord it over us, He came to love us and to serve us. When we experience that kind of love, not in our heads but in our hearts, it becomes a joy to serve other people. You can see that in the geometry of the cross. God pouring down all of His love, all of His blessings onto us, so that we can then reach out and serve others in His name.

Jesus transformed the world not with an army, not with a government, not by lording it over people. Jesus transformed the world with a basin and a towel. He invites us to be part of that on-going transformation of the world, as we serve others in His name. And whether we know it or not, deep, deep down, this is what we most long to do.

This is what we were designed to do. Nobody hopes that at their funeral someone will stand up and say, "Yes, he worked real hard, and he was anxious and self-occupied a lot. But he sure knew how to get a lot of stuff in life." None of us want that said at our memorial. All of us hope that someone will stand up and say, "My life is richer, my world is bigger, and my faith is stronger, because this person walked the planet. She made a difference. He changed my life." We don't want to be space takers, we don't want to be resume builders, we want to be difference makers, and know that we have significance. And the good news we celebrate, is that Jesus came, not to judge us, but to show us how much

He loved us, so that in response to that we can give ourselves away in service to the world, and know the joy He promises comes from doing that.

From Evening to Morning
Let's move on from John 13 to John 21 - the breakfast Jesus had with His special friends after His resurrection.

There's a story that teachers just love to tell about four students who decided to skip a mid-term exam and go surfing instead. When they got back, they lied to the tutor and said that the reason they missed the exam was because on the way to class they got a flat tyre. They asked if they could have a make-up exam. The tutor said, "Flat tyre, huh?" Sounded suspicious to him, but he said, "Okay, go ahead and come back tomorrow." So the next day they came back, and the tutor put them in four separate rooms so they couldn't talk to each other. When they opened the test, there was only one question on it: "Which tyre?" I have no idea if that story is true or not, but teachers love to tell it. Those students had blown it big time. What do you do when you blow it? When you make a mistake at work, do you 'fess up? Or try to hide it? Or maybe try to pin the blame on someone else? Or when you yell at your children too much, do you apologise? Or comfort yourself by thinking how much they richly deserved it? Not to mention the whoppers we manage to commit along the way: the times we say something wounding to a friend; or when we're workaholics and end up wrecking our families.

What do you do when you've blown it? For three years Jesus had been Peter's best friend. For three years Jesus had been there for Peter at every turn. When Peter's mother-in-law was sick, Jesus healed her. When Peter was in a small boat being battered by a storm, Jesus calmed the storm and taught Peter how to walk on water. Jesus even gave Peter his new name, Peter, which means, the rock. But then the one moment when Jesus needed Peter, when Jesus was on trial for His life, Peter caved like a house of cards, and not only refused to help Jesus, but pretended that he didn't even know Jesus. Not once, not twice, but three times, he denied knowing Jesus.

Just a few hours earlier Peter had been filled with such big words. He was bragging. He said, "Jesus, I'll never leave you. These other guys, they might leave you. Just look at them, the worthless lot. But not me. I'll never leave you Jesus. What you need to understand is, I'm your boy.

You stick with me, Jesus, I'll take you places." But then, just a few hours later, Peter denied knowing Him at all. And even though Jesus had been raised from the dead, and even though Jesus' death pays the penalty for every wrong thing we've ever done, Peter still did not believe that all of the talk about forgiveness, and grace, and second chances were for him. Grace was for everybody else, but he was a loser, and there are no second chances for losers.

So Peter says one of the most heart-breaking things in the whole Bible: "I'm going fishing." That is one of the loneliest lines in Scripture. Peter is saying, "I didn't do this disciple thing right. I have blown it big time. I'm going fishing. Back to what I know. I'm going to run away from my problems. I'm going to pretend it didn't even happen. I'm going fishing."

Do you ever do that? Do you ever run away, especially when you've blown it? Maybe you've hurt a friend and you don't want to deal with it, you don't know how to deal with it, so you just start avoiding that person? Or maybe your marriage goes south and you say, "You know what? I'm giving up. Can't fix this." Maybe you go and find someone else. Or when you blow it, do you escape into shopping, or alcohol, or work, or entertainment, or sports, or whatever it is? But what is so compelling about the God that is revealed in Jesus, and only the God that is revealed in Jesus, is the way that He handles Peter's failure in this story, and then by extension the way God handles our failures.

1) JESUS LOVINGLY CONFRONTS US.

Not to make us feel guilty, but so that He can forgive us and give us a second chance, because you can't be forgiven unless you first admit you've got a problem, and you've done something wrong. So Jesus confronts us. In this story, Jesus doesn't come up to Peter and say, "So, anyway Peter, as I was saying before you betrayed me..." as if nothing was wrong. Jesus knows there's an issue and it needs to be dealt with.

Jesus confronts us in a lot of different ways. Sometimes it's through that inner voice of the Holy Spirit that doesn't make us feel guilty but that does reveal our sin to us and then gives us the hope that if we turn to Jesus we'll be forgiven. And then sometimes Jesus confronts us through our circumstances. In this story, Peter has been fishing all night and he hasn't caught a thing, which is my kind of fishing. Jesus comes along, and says, "Do you have any fish?" Basically, Jesus is saying, "How's this running away thing working out for you Peter? Is it doing you any good?" It's a reminder that the things we run to when we want to avoid our problems, whether it's shopping, or alcohol, or work, those things usually don't do any good, and often they just do a lot of harm. So Jesus confronts us with our sin so that we can get better.

But we hate that, don't we? We don't want to be confronted when we've done something wrong. When we've blown it, we want to forget about it. We don't want to admit unpleasant truths about ourselves. I think this is a cultural deal. We hate saying that we're wrong, we hate admitting anything unpleasant, as a matter of fact. As a culture, we just want to avoid all that stuff. Just look at all the euphemisms we have in our culture. Notice how nobody gets fired anymore? They're let go. It almost sounds like a good thing. "Were you fired?" "No, I was let go." "Oh good for you. You don't want to be held down." Or my favourite: "Pre-owned cars." Oh come on. You know that that means this thing was owned by ten different owners that never changed the oil so don't come crying to us when it breaks down.

That's what we do with our sin. We down-play, we minimise, we hide it, we pretend we didn't do it. But you can't get better unless you admit you've got a problem.

A father was teaching his four year old son how to roller skate. At one point the little boy crashed to the ground. His dad said, "What happened?" His son said a very profound thing. He said, *"I fell down."* Very powerful. He didn't give excuses. He didn't say it was because of bad parenting, inadequate training, or that he was a victim of gravity. He said, "I fell down." A simple statement.

Do you think you could do that? Let's just practice for a moment. Repeat after me: "I blew it." If you said it – *and how would I know!* Well - it wasn't that hard, was it? To admit you're wrong is just another way of saying you know more now than you used to. In order to heal us, Jesus confronts us, and our job is to admit our sin.

2) JESUS REALISTICALLY FACES US.

In this story, Peter should be out preaching. But Jesus meets Peter in his place of escape, in the place to which he's running away, in his place of shame and sin. That's what Jesus does.

A man had an addiction to internet pornography for years, but then he started to get this sense of Jesus in the room with him every time he was looking at porn. Eventually it got stronger and stronger, and he said he could almost physically feel Jesus sitting right next to him, not to judge him, and certainly not approving of what he was doing, but just sitting next to him saying, "I have so much more for you than this." He said that killed it. All that grace, all that love, in the middle of his sin, he couldn't take it anymore, he quit. He got over the addiction.

Unlike every other god in every other religion, the God revealed in Jesus does not ask us to clean ourselves up before we can go to Him. He comes to us, even in the middle of the ugliest parts of our lives, and our job when He does that, is to enter into relationship with Him.

3) JESUS THOROUGHLY FORGIVES US.

I know we hear that all the time, Jesus forgives us; it's sort of an intellectual, theological thing we've got in our brain. But Jesus didn't mean forgiveness to be an intellectual concept. Jesus meant it to be an earthshaking life altering cataclysmic experience. In this story, Jesus doesn't want Peter just to understand that he's forgiven. He wants Peter to have an experience in his heart, not in his head, of being thoroughly and completely forgiven.

That's why Jesus doesn't give a little sermon on forgiveness here. Instead, He gives Peter an experience. If you look at the story closely, what Jesus is doing is walking Peter through their entire three year friendship, so that Peter can experience his forgiveness. Peter and Jesus first met three years earlier when Peter had been out fishing all night. In that story too, he hadn't caught anything. You kind of wonder why he was a fisherman; he didn't seem to do it very well. But Jesus comes along and provides him a miraculous catch of fish. That's how they met. So in this story, Jesus reenacts the way they met. In this story, Jesus makes a meal of bread and fish, which Peter has seen before, when Jesus fed 5,000 people with just those same two ingredients.

When Peter denied Jesus, Peter was standing by a charcoal fire, so in this story Jesus builds a charcoal fire. Jesus is taking Peter through their entire friendship so that Peter can experience Jesus' forgiveness, not just know about it. Then Jesus says this interesting thing to Peter. He says, "Peter, do you love me more than *these*?" What did Jesus mean by the word, '*these*'? Nobody knows. Some people say, "Well, Jesus is referring to the other disciples." Or some people say, "Maybe Jesus was referring to the fish." Which seems unlikely, don't you think? "Peter, do you love me more than fish?" "Yes, Lord, but not as much as fish and chips!" It makes no sense!

Jesus meant it to be unclear. Jesus is saying, "Do you love me more than anything that can fit in this unclear pronoun reference here?" Do you love me more than anything?

The Greek in this story is very important. As you may know, there are different words for the word "love" in Greek. There's "agape" which is the highest form of love, that's the sacrificial, committed kind of love. And then there's "philio" which is more of a friendship or affection. In this story, Jesus twice says to Peter, "Do you agape me?" The highest form of love. But Peter says, "Well, I philio you." So then the last time, the third time, Jesus changes His word, and He says, "Okay Peter, well then, do you philio me?" As if Jesus were saying, "Okay Peter, if the best you can do is philio, that's good enough for me right now, we'll get to agape later."

Which Peter eventually did. He eventually loved Jesus so much he was willing to be crucified upside down for knowing Him. By asking this question three times, Jesus was giving Peter a chance to say "I love you, Lord" three times, erasing his three denials. It is a thorough, complete experience of forgiveness.

Question of Experience

Have you ever had that experience with Jesus? Have you ever experienced Jesus' forgiveness, or is it just head knowledge for you? I would invite you to daily pray, "Jesus, give me an experience, not a theology of your grace, Jesus give me an experience of your grace." Pray for that. Maybe even in your mind, go back to those moments of failure, and shame, and sin that you try to deny. Go back to those moments, just like Jesus takes Peter back to those moments in this story, and then in prayer, ask the Holy Spirit to help you imagine what Jesus would say to you in those moments of failure, so that you can have an experience of His forgiveness, not just head knowledge.

When we've blown it – Jesus confronts us so we can grow. He meets us where we are, not where we should be. He gives us an experience of forgiveness.

4) JESUS CONFIDENTLY COMMISSIONS US.

Jesus says to Peter in this story, "Peter, feed my sheep." In other words, he gives Peter a job to do. This is important because what He's saying to Peter is, "You're not just forgiven, Peter. You still have a place in my kingdom. You still have a purpose. I still have confidence in you, even though you've blown it." It would be as if you wrecked your dad's car when you were a kid, and your dad went out and bought a brand new car and let you drive it right off the lot.

You'd know that even though you blew it, your Dad still had confidence in you. Or had really good insurance. One of the two. But let's go with confidence. Jesus is saying, "Peter, I know you think you've blown it beyond repair. I know you think that because you've messed up you have no worth, any value, nothing to offer. I know you think you're a poser and a pretender. But I once called you the rock upon which I would build my church, and that is still true, Peter. You are still that rock, you are still my man, Peter. You are still my man. You are not a pretender, you are Rocky. So get back in the game because I'm not giving up on you, so don't you give up on yourself either."

Peter has spent three years learning to believe in Jesus, and what he discovers is how much Jesus believes in him. With Jesus, failure is never fatal.

It's a little bit like those commercials that you hear for various financial things. You know how at the end the legal man, who talks even faster than I talk, he comes on, and he always says the same thing: "Past performance does not guarantee future results." In other words, "If this stock tanks, don't sue me, because I didn't promise you the world." Now, in the financial world, that phrase is a warning. In the Kingdom of God, it's a promise. Even when you blow it, your past performance in no way predicts your future results. In spite of how badly you've messed up, you still have a future, God still has a job for you, He still has confidence in you, and our job is to ask in prayer, "Lord, what's my assignment? Send me back into your kingdom. Send me back into your battle."

Because, with Jesus, even when we blow it, past performance does not predict future results.

So where might you have blown it lately? Will you pray this week, “Lord, show me my sin.” And then, will you admit it, and let Jesus forgive you, and give you a job to do in his kingdom, so you can know that He still has confidence in you. Or maybe you know someone who’s blown it lately, and how can you help them experience Jesus’ forgiveness and His restoration, so that you, and all of those around you will know with certainty, the good news that in Jesus even when you blow it, past performance in no way predicts future results.

Let’s pray about this - *Lord, thank you for this amazing truth. We ask that you would help us live in it, and respond to it, and we’ll give you all the glory. We pray this in your name, Jesus. Amen.*

Life Summary?

Have you ever read a saying that seems to perfectly sum up your life? I did in an Email. Someone wrote about various sayings and this one stood out above all the rest. It read simply: "I never make *MiSakes*!" (That’s spelt without a *T* – *misakes* not *mistakes* – get it?)

That little saying is perfect for my life, because it shows my inability to get some things right no matter how hard I try or how simple they seem to be. It goes beyond the mistakes in spelling and grammar you often find in my writings, I may have trouble getting things right in almost any area of my life.

Like you I try, I really try to do things in the best possible way, but sometimes no matter how much I try I just can't do it. Each morning I pray that God will lead me and give me the wisdom to recognise His leading. I pray that He will give me wisdom to make the right decisions in my daily life and in the areas where my life touches the lives of others.

The truth is though, that I do make mistakes! In fact it seems that if you or I were keeping account I would have more mistakes than positive successes.

You may be like me, but I hope you do a better job at life than I! If however you are like me you may be wondering "What's the use," "Why even try?" Because I make mistakes! I say the wrong things, I do the wrong thing, I have the wrong thoughts and I tend to keep account of those things in my own heart (which is another mistake).

The apostle John wrote in 1 John: "If we say we have no sin, (never make a mistake) we are only fooling ourselves and refusing to accept the truth. But if we confess our sins to him, he is faithful and just to forgive us and to cleanse us from every wrong."

Realising that we are all bound to have weaknesses is not an excuse to stop trying to do what is right. It does not justify our intentional involvement in disobedience to God's word.

John also writes: "If someone says, 'I belong to God,' but doesn't obey God's commandments, that person is a liar and does not live in the truth. But those who obey God's Word really do love Him. That is the way to know whether or not we live in Him. Those who say they live in God should live their lives as Christ did."

The bottom line is this: No matter how badly we mess up trying to live for God, no matter how many mistakes we make, God will forgive us, if we truly want to obey His words.

If we can say, "I never make *miSakes*" - and know that even as you say it it's not so. Go through it in your mind prayerfully – the meal that Jesus made for people like Peter who failed Him and let Him down.

Don't live with regrets. Peter became a servant of Christ and preached to thousands on the Day of Pentecost. Life was different, better and for real. It can be for us.

(5) GLORY IN US

The question is this: *What it is that God really wants for us more than anything else? What is He really after for us?*

There is just one proper answer to that – its God's biggest aim throughout all of history to make a big display of His own GLORY.

Whether it's in what He has created in the world and universe. Whether it's in the redemption of His people. Or whether it's in growing us to be more like Him in attitude and action. There's one thing we can know for sure about God and it's this. God has an overwhelming passion and zeal and energy for His OWN GLORY. In us that would sound bad. In God it's right as I want us to see.

There's nothing beyond this for us. The glory of God is the terminus of everything for us. I don't suppose it has been put any better than when the Scottish Catechism says, *"Man's chief end is to glorify God."* That's the top goal of living. That's the great business of our lives.

Life's Purpose
It's so important for us to know what makes life 'tick'. We want to understand how things work. God made us with a scientific outlook.

A child will want to know, "What's that for?" "Or why did it do that, dad?" To which he might reply, *"Ask your mother!"* But here's the question we have to face – Have we discovered what we are for? *'Man's chief end is to glorify God, and to enjoy Him for ever.'*

2 Corinthians 3:7-18 makes this so clear. God the Father, God the Son and God the Holy Spirit are totally taken up with this.

This is what the **FATHER** is doing in creation – both in the animate and the inanimate creation. *He is displaying His glory*. In the created order of the universe, what's the universe doing? *"The heavens declare the glory of God; the earth is full of His glory,"* says Isaiah.

When God made man, what was His purpose? He made man in His image to bear His likeness, and Hebrews tells us that **WE** are **CROWNED** with glory.

This is what the Son is taken up with in His birth, life and death. At His birth, men said that they *saw* and *gazed* at His glory – this glory revealed that He was the one and only Son of the Father. He was full of grace and truth.

In His LIFE what was He doing? He spoke of glorifying God's Name and finishing the work He had for Him to do. What about Christ's DEATH? He spoke of God being glorified through His death.

Do you see why I write that the glory of God is the overwhelming preoccupation of the FATHER in creation, of the SON in redemption, and also the aim of the HOLY SPIRIT in making us what we God wants us to be?

As Paul writes, *"We, who with unveiled faces all reflect the Lord's glory, are being transformed into his likeness with ever-increasing glory, which comes from the Lord, who is the Spirit" (2 Cor.3:18).*

Do you see the staggering truth presented here? God created the world like a *theatre* in which to display His *glory.* He has sent His SON in order that we may see something of His glory in the face of Jesus Christ – He is now working by the Holy Spirit in the hearts and lives of His people that they may be changed into the image of His glory.

The Glory of God

Now to properly know what this means let me make clear what the Bible is meaning by the *'glory'* of God.

The original meaning of the word *'glory'* in the Bible is really *weight.* And that's *weight* in the sense of the *heaviness* of something. So it came to mean someone's worth – what they were worthy of; and by implication, their *character.* The glory of God is the display of His worth, of His character.

This is why we see the glory of God as supremely displayed in the Cross of Jesus. This is why Jesus prayed immediately before His death, "Father Glorify Your Son." The Cross of Jesus is a display of the Glory of God.

John Calvin made this point: *"Nowhere in the universe does God display His glory more fully than in the Cross of Christ."*

It's because there the wisdom, love, justice, mercy, goodness and faithfulness of God are on show in all that God has done.

It makes we who believe, part of the people called the FORGIVEN MUCH. When we understand that, we will love much and will serve much, and worship much, and adore Him, out of a heart of devotion and not just do it because we're 'Christians' and we're meant to do that kind of thing.

Pastor and Author Joe Stowell tells of a meeting at the great Moody church in Chicago. The Brooklyn Tabernacle choir were singing that night. He said, "Here were 180 people from Brooklyn, New York singing in Chicago and they're not professional singers. These are addicts and former prostitutes who have been redeemed. I'll never forget the moment, when the light went down and the spotlight hit the choir and they sang their first great song of the GLORY of the redeeming work of Jesus Christ. I saw something I'd never seen in a choir before. As they began to sing, the spots were catching the glistening tears that were running down the cheeks of those singing the GLORY of the gospel in Jesus Christ."

He made this comment which I'm sure some of you will nod your heads in agreement to – "I felt cheated because I'm a *lifer*. I was saved when I was SIX, so I was saved from things like biting my sister and not picking up my toys. Sometimes it's hard for us *lifers* to get a grip on how much we've been forgiven for. And in the midst of my feeling cheated, it was as though the Holy Spirit began to work me over and said, 'Joe, did you ever think of where you might be, if I had not rescued you at six? Did you ever think of where your lust might have taken you, if my Spirit hadn't been bringing along self-control? Have you ever thought about where your greed would have taken you, if I hadn't been schooling you in generosity? Where your self-centredness would have taken you if I had not been teaching you the love of others? Did you ever?' Then it dawned on me; thank God I am among the forgiven much. I owe such a debt and so do you."

We do, don't we? God shows His glory in the Cross. This is also why the glory of God is shown in God's LAW – since it's a reflection of His character.

And it's this that Paul is illustrating from, in the earlier part of 2 Corinthians 3.

Do you remember in Exodus 34, when Moses went to Mount Sinai, and God instructed him to inscribe the law on stone tablets, when he came down from Sinai to the people, his face shone? The apostle refers to that in verse 7: *"Now if the ministry that brought death, which was engraved in letters on stone, came with glory, so that the Israelites could not look steadily at the face of Moses because of its glory, fading though it was."*

It's because there the wisdom, love, justice, mercy, goodness, and the faithfulness of God are displayed in all that God has done. He displays His glory in the Cross.

This is the reason why God's glory is displayed in His law. What is His law? It's a reflection of God's character. It's this that Paul is illustrating from in the earlier part of 2 Corinthians 3.

Moses' face shone. Now why? Because the law of God is an expression of God's character – and the glory of God flamed out on that mountain, and Moses' face reflected the glory.

That was an amazing sight. All of God's people were awed by the sight. But – Paul is saying this – God has something so much more wonderful, so much more amazing and staggering to do now. This is a new time with a new covenant by God, and He intends to show off His glory again, but not on *stone* but in *people* – the lives and characters of His children.

A Comparison

Do you see how Paul is drawing a comparison for us? Just take a moment to see a contrast between the two ways.

The glory of the old covenant was in its exclusiveness – it was for Moses alone. Nobody else's face shone with this glory. It was particular. But the glory of the new covenant in Christ is *inclusive*.

"And we, who with unveiled faces all reflect the Lord's glory, are being transformed." That means there's not one of us who need be left out. In our lives the glory of God can appear in our character. This is God's aim for us all. It's inclusive not exclusive.

The glory of the old covenant was temporary but this glory is *permanent.*

Paul says, *"And if what was fading away came with glory, how much greater is the glory of that which lasts! Therefore, since we have such a hope, we are very bold. We are not like Moses, who would put a veil over his face to keep the Israelites from gazing at it while the radiance was fading away"* (2 Cor.3:11). It was a fading glory, not permanent. But look at verse 18. The glory which the Holy Spirit is seeking to work into our character is a glory which will last and increase. *"We are being transformed into his likeness with ever-increasing glory."*

Even more than that – Back in the days of Moses it was an outward and a physical reflection, whereas this glory the Holy Spirit creates in us is an inward spiritual transformation. It's not that we just reflect God's glory – we are going to be changed into the same image. It's the same word that is used of Jesus' transfiguration. It's the word from which we get our word *metamorphosis.*

On the Mount of Transfiguration the disciples looked on with utter amazement at what was happening to Jesus. Peter really didn't know what to say other than to want to stay there. The glory of God was shining right through Him. It defied description. God has a transfiguration to accomplish in us so that we're changed into the same image.

Manifested Glory
There are three areas in which the Bible tells us that the *glory* of the Lord Jesus Christ is manifest.

One is in the PAST – it's manifest in history. Another is in the FUTURE – It will be manifest in eternity, and we look towards that day when we shall see Him as He is in glory. But between history and eternity God's glory is to be manifest in us – *IN YOU AND ME!*

Isn't that amazing? It's staggering as a truth. The question is how does this work?
Let me underline three things verse 18 makes clear about this –

1) THE SOURCE OF GOD'S GLORY INDWELLING.

This inner work of transfiguration is the great ministry of the indwelling Holy Spirit. It comes from the Spirit. It doesn't belong to anything that we can do. It's the sole prerogative of God the Holy Spirit – to transform our characters that they might be radiant with the very glory of God.

People like to talk about experiencing the Holy Spirit. But let's make sure that we don't get side-tracked. The main job of the Holy Spirit is to work from the *inside* out to change us into the *image* of the Lord Jesus, so that He may be glorified through us.

What The Holy Spirit Does

That's what the Holy Spirit's basic ministry is. This is the only genuine mark of the Holy Spirit at work in us. We mustn't get diverted by anything from this. The Holy Spirit above all else wants to transform our inner character. And there's no substitute for it. It's what He does when He fills us. The Spirit of the living God has all the power of the Godhead at His disposal.

We do a real injustice to God's greatness and majesty when we limit His power, and the possibilities of His power, in our own minds. One of the great things about being in Christian ministry is seeing God's power by the Holy Spirit taking broken and spoiled people and making them into new people. It's fantastic to see how God etches into their lives something of the glory and beauty of Jesus.

Strength for Today and Tomorrow

This is what gives us the strength to go on. We're living in a disillusioning day. Life is full of the mundane, the drudgery, and the grey and depressing. For the Christian the future is really bright with hope because the best is yet to be. But I think we often misunderstand what the authentic Christian life is all about.

Godliness is viewed in a person as a kind of negative, austere, cold, and unapproachable attitude. It's the person who belongs to the stained-glass window set. They don't live in the real world. A genuine work of the Holy Spirit, when the glory of God begins to appear through a person – it makes that person more human, not less human. We don't say of such a person, *"Oh, I could never go to him. They're too holy, I couldn't approach them."* There's a fire in the glory of God that not only burns but warms and draws people into God's love. It's this way that people are set free to be truly human and truly natural. We can never be all that we're meant to be until God's Spirit begins His work in us.

VISIBLE GLORY

Not merely in the words you say,
Not only in your deeds confessed,
But in the most unconscious way
Is Christ expressed?

Is it a beatific smile,
A holy light upon your brow?
Oh, no, I felt His presence
When you laughed just now.

And from your eyes He beckons me,
And from your heart His love is shed,
Till I lose sight of you and see
The Christ instead.

The beauty of a restored humanity. This work is **SOURCED** by the Holy Spirit.

2) THE SECRET OF GOD'S GLORY EXPERIENCED.

"We, who with unveiled faces all reflect the Lord's glory, are being transformed into his likeness with ever-increasing glory."

We are transformed when we reflect the Lord's glory. What does this mean and how does it work? According to Charles Hodge, the great Bible commentator – this means, NOT what will happen when we get to be with Christ in heaven – that will be glory indeed *but of a different kind to this.* This is the glory that comes now through God's Word and by His Holy Spirit.

The thing that the Holy Spirit constantly wants to do is to bring glory to Christ. And therefore the Holy Spirit will start transforming us in our characters as we give ourselves to concentrating on the Word of God.

We need to meditate on it, study it and let the truth of it absorb us. In this way we start to know God.

The secret of our transformation is to see where God has revealed Himself. God has shown Himself in HIS WORD – and we need to remind ourselves that this is what the Bible is for. Our Bible is a revelation of God that we might come to know Him.

God hasn't given us His Word so that we might have a few pleasant thoughts to comfort and inspire our day – although, thank God if it does that for us.

The whole point of the Bible is for God to show us Himself, to get us used to His purposes, that we might come to know Him, and be changed into His likeness.

Picture This

A *youthful face* framed by a head of hair whiter than a great grandfather. *Bronzed feet* like those of a statue that supports an otherwise human-looking form of flesh and bones. *Blinding*, supernatural light shooting forth from unblinking eyes. A *dagger-like* weapon of bright, burnished metal that protrudes from the mouth of this un-earthly visitor.

Is this the latest horror movie? Is it a character in a virtual reality game teenagers like to play these days? No it's not – maybe you recognised where I was going with that description. It's the vision described by John in Revelation 1. It's John's vision of JESUS, GOD THE WORD, after His ascension into heaven.

That vision really got to John. The thing that seems to have piqued his interest the most is that the voice he heard was associated with a SWORD protruding from the Messiah's mouth. Comparing this vision with other passages of Scripture, we discover the meaning of this amazing symbol of the SWORD. It represents nothing less than God's penetratingly powerful words coming out from the mouth of the One who had been crucified, but who rose again, and who is now at the right hand of the Father.

What is as sharp as a two-edged sword yet as thunderous as an ocean's waves relentlessly pounding upon the shore? When John heard the *voice* of Jesus, he testified that it was 'as the sound of many waters'. As the waves crashed unceasingly upon the cliffs of Patmos, so the sound of His Master's words came flooding in his consciousness. He couldn't help but perceive the clear, unmistakable words of the Lord of the universe.

Hebrews 4:12 tells us that *"The Word of God is living and powerful, and sharper than any two-edged sword."* Ephesians 6:17, *"The sword of the Spirit, which is the word of God."*

We must never forget this – the Bible, that is the written Word of God, is in reality just as much an extension of Jesus' person as the sword that John saw protruding from Jesus' mouth.

He who existed in the beginning as the Word of God faithfully spoke God's words while He lived on Earth. Those words have now been miraculously conveyed to us in written form by the effective working of the Holy Spirit.

An Extension

In other words – the relationship between the Bible and its author is closer than we may imagine. Precisely because God's written Word is an extension of Jesus Christ, we can count on it being true. Not only that, it's also a sure-fire way that we can check the validity of any other medium through whom God may choose to make Himself known today.

The only issue is what is His Word really saying? And we can know the truth if we truly submit our will to our Heavenly Father. Please note that nowhere in John's vision, or anywhere else in the Scriptures for that matter, are we encouraged to make an idol out of the *sword.* We're never exhorted to worship the Bible as 'special' in itself.

Think of it like this – I have a physical tongue which serves to communicate my thought to you right now. So – the *two-edged sword* that proceeds from the mouth of Jesus, now in written form, is how He chooses to express Himself in this era of grace.

Yes, my tongue is alive, but if it were cut off from me, it would become a dead and useless thing. In other words, my tongue has no meaning or purpose apart from me. Because I live, it has life.

The Bottom Line

Because JESUS lives, the BIBLE lives. Our Lord has commissioned us to be agents of the Bible's incalculable treasures.

Question

Why did He take so great a chance with fallible people like us? It's painfully obvious that we certainly need the Word of God as never before. And that's why the Lord went to such huge lengths to preserve it for us. The Word of God is to be to our soul and spirit what physical sustenance is to the body.

For us as believers it's to be like manna, our daily bread. Moreover, it's a finely polished mirror that gives us a faithful reflection of who we really are when identified with Christ. Countless millions have testified that the Bible has been a healing balm that soothes the nerves and calms our temperament, bringing comfort in the middle of life's greatest pains and sorrows. There's no doubt that we need the Word of God as never before – but is that reason enough for the Lord of creation to entrust it to the likes of you and me?

Wouldn't it have been far better if He had, for example, committed it to the angels to do with as they saw fit? God doesn't do that. He gives His Word to us.

But do you see – what does that tell us about the One whom we call Lord? What a Saviour! What a Lord! He became a man to remain a man forever in order that He might become *'the firstborn among many brethren.'* He did what He did because He delights in being our Brother – our *big* Brother who watches over and takes care of His family – our big Brother who wants to encourage us. Our big Brother who wants to impart to us the confidence that as we trust the Father, we, too, can accomplish everything that God has called us to do.

Our Brother has committed Himself to us completely and unreservedly. He not only *loves* us, but He *likes* us and desires our company and fellowship forever – yours and mine. To top it all, He gives us the opportunity of being agents over the very things that He suffered and died for!

We are the appointed managers of the mysteries of heaven and earth. He entrusts not only HIS WORD, but His SPIRIT, His reputation, His very being, to His blood-bought family.

Let's allow this to get a grip on us – The Word of God still sets the captive free, and by its radiance countless roads are being illumined.

God's Word can make even the simplest of men and women to be as wise as Solomon. And wise men and women seek the Saviour through the pages of a Book – a Book held and treasured and applied. This is God's appointed means for changing us into His own image.

A lady ended up with her life in small pieces, not knowing how to put *Humpty Dumpty together again.* I think she came to a church meeting as a last resort thinking something magical might happen to her so that she would get the answer for her needs. She was really disappointed when told to keep coming to church and keep listening to God's Word, that was what will change her. She did keep going and she kept herself under God's Word letting it pour over her. That woman became transformed – she is changed beyond recognition.

Someone will say, *"That's all very well, but I don't have that kind of ministry to sit under."* I know that may be the case. But better than that – God knows it to be the case. However, if we have a genuine hunger we will find a way. There are recordings and lots of different ways to expose ourselves to God's Word.

We can't get around it – the SECRET for the transforming glory of God to break through is from times in HIS WORD.

But there's *another means* God's Holy Spirit uses to change us into this same image. Paul tells us that something else happens that gets this glory. He writes: *"Our light and momentary troubles are achieving for us an eternal glory that far outweighs them all"* (2 Cor.4:17). There's a connection between the TESTING and the TRIALS we go through as God's people, and the glory that God is seeking to produce in us.

To the Romans Paul made a similar point. He said that he didn't reckon that the suffering right now was worth comparing to the glory to come.

Trial and Glory

Trials, in God's hands can become a means to glory. I find it interesting that Paul said to the church at Philippi, *"I've learned to experience Jesus in the midst of sufferings."*

There are only three types of people. Those who *have* experienced suffering. Those who *are* experiencing it, and those who *will.*

We don't like trials. We certainly don't have to say, *"Okay Lord, bring them on."* But do ask for wisdom from the Lord so that we don't waste the trials that do come. It's an important moment for you to have a shared experience with Jesus Christ.

Of course you want the trial to leave. I hope it does leave – but until it does, could you say to Jesus, "Lord, I never ever knew before what it meant for You to love me because now I feel the loneliness **YOU** must have felt on that Cross for me. I want to meet You here. I want to share in Your experience. I love You. You volunteered loneliness for me. Lord, I hate being betrayed by my friends. But, Lord, how You must have felt in that garden when You started toward the Cross for me."

Paul says – *"When suffering comes my way, I meet Jesus there and I share in the fellowship. I experience Jesus in a way I've never experienced Him before."*

The SOURCE of our changing is the HOLY SPIRIT.
The SECRET is through His *SCRIPTURES* and *SUFFERING* –

3) THE SERIES OF GOD GLORY EXPERIENCES

It's not something that happens overnight or in a week. It's the work of a lifetime. We are *being transformed* – it's in the present tense – a *continuous* looking produces a *continuous* transfiguration. That work goes on from the start of our Christian life all the way through to when we see our Lord face to face.

Have you noticed that when the New Testament writers comment on holiness and Christlikeness, they always use *biological* and *horticultural* metaphors? Its *birth* and *growth*. it's *sowing* and *reaping*. These are the terms in which our Bible speaks of our growing in holiness and in grace.

Crisis Moments?
This doesn't mean there are no crisis moments for us. We may have a crisis to face – a crisis of *repentance*, a crisis of *new obedience*; a crisis of a *truth* suddenly hitting home. But these crises are like surgical operations which make health and growth possible, not unnecessary.

There is no blessing of any kind that we can have which will make it unnecessary for us to go on growing in grace, by God's appointed methods. So we ought to be saying (as the writer to the Hebrews put it) *"Let us go on. Let nothing hinder the growth curve. Let's go on and become like the Lord."*

Our world is in desperate trouble.

VISIBLE GLORY

People are in real trouble. God will not be content until He takes us from glory to Glory, and meanwhile, until His face shows up through ours.

I'm reminded of a man in prison because of His faith in Christ. He shared a cell with a man with no faith – cynical, hard as nails and embittered by the injustice of his imprisonment and daily hardships. He couldn't help noticing the attitude of his cell-mate – the Christ-like attitude and actions that he displayed. The strength of character and peace of mind despite the trials he was going through - just as bad as his own and some days worse. There came a day when he turned to the Christian and said, *"What is your Jesus like? Because if Jesus is like YOU, I want to know Him."*

Don't we want that? It comes when it's the passion of our lives to experience Christ, to have a real closeness to Him. This isn't for other people – it's for us! Make Him the passionate pursuit, meeting Him.

One day we will see Him.
Oh that will be glory for me,
Glory for me, glory for me.
When by His grace
I shall look on His face,
That will be glory, be glory for me.
Let's bring that day nearer by what we are right now.

(6) GLORY COMING DOWN

GLORY IN US was the topic in the last chapter and now we are moving on to GLORY COMING DOWN. All will be explained through a focus on an amazing prayer of the prophet Isaiah in chapter 64.

This was said by a Church Pastor. He teaches several thousand people every Sunday. He was brutally honest when he said this: *"I'm already getting tired of me. I'm getting tired of those insecurities that have dogged me my whole life, that I try to climb on top of, the insecurities that haunt my spirit almost every single day. I'm tired of those failures that I think I've got on top of and then there they are again, nipping at my soul. I get tired of that, tired of feeling uncomfortable in some situations that I ought to know how to deal with. But I'm here to tell you another thing. After all these years, I still have not grown tired of Jesus. I find Him today more compelling, more awesome, more adventuresome, more wonderful, more follow-able, more sometimes wonderfully troubling, and more surprising than I have ever found Him in my life. I find that I never get tired of Jesus. And I've also discovered that if life is all about me, it can't be about Him. And if it's going to be all about Him then it can be nothing of me; I've discovered you can't have it both ways. And if I have to make a choice, I'll choose a life that's all about Jesus. I find such satisfaction in that."*

Those words of JOE STOWELL spoken at the English Keswick Convention are so true - and I find a real echo in my own life. That's one reason why I'm writing this book to help us to wallow in the glory of the Lord Jesus Christ.

I travelled to Israel with a group and taught the gospels as we moved around. I well remember going to the Qumran area near to the Dead Sea and scrambling around the rocks. A little later I stood in the Shrine of the Book in Jerusalem, where the entire scroll of ISAIAH recovered from the Dead Sea caves at Qumran is the focus.

The Book of Isaiah is rooted in history but there's more to it than that, which is why I want to take a few moments now focusing on the message this great Old Testament prophet proclaimed. Isaiah is coming to the end of a long ministry. With prophetic eye he looks into the future and sees the terrible judgments which he had been told to pronounce against Israel now beginning to be fulfilled. It was hard enough getting the message in the first place let alone seeing them underlined – these things would happen.

What does Isaiah see?
Isaiah sees how the people of Israel will languish for years in Babylon until the 70 years of their exile from their land have almost dragged their course. So deeply does he feel for the captives that the cry he utters is just the same as the cry he wants them to make when that day comes – so much so that the great Theologian Charles Simeon describes Isaiah 64 as *"A prayer drawn up by the prophet for the use of the Jews when they should be in captivity in Babylon."*

Sometimes facing a crisis it's helpful to have some words we can use in prayer to God – words other than – *"Oh my God!"* or, *"Help me out of this by getting me out of here!"* Facing really tough times there in captivity they couldn't have found a more appropriate prayer to pray in their bondage – and nor can we when we feel today's Church is going through tough times because of our wrong. For we just *must* think about ourselves and our church situation – the needs that we have, the sense that we're away from the blessings of God and all bound up and limited in what we want to see happening. Of course we're not in *physical* slavery – but at a spiritual level the church can most certainly face the restraining of God's Spirit – we can feel we're not where we would like to be as His people.

An Inhibited Life
Years ago I remember reading a prayer from a young man – *"Lord, save me from an inhibited life."* He had an honest point to make not just about himself but lots of other church-going people. We don't always enjoy an authentic freedom of God by His Spirit doing things in and through us that we know is part of the true Christian life.

A Relevant Prayer
There's often a compromise about our behaviour and powerlessness in our actions. Frankly – I don't know a prayer that's more relevant to our situation than Isaiah 64. It's Isaiah's last recorded prayer for His people. And look at what he does – he pours all the pent-up yearning of his heart.

The prayer really starts at 63:7 by a recollection of God's PAST mercies – that's the best way to start our prayers. Then he follows up by appealing to God to look at their PRESENT pitiable state. Then he follows up with a fervent and yet reasoned appeal to God personally to step in for His glory's sake – and that's the best way to conclude our prayers.

From Isaiah 64:1 his prayer has four parts – there's **INTENSITY** about it. There's Isaiah's **INVOLVEMENT** – he doesn't say *they* are at fault – he includes himself personally. Next, there's an **INCENTIVE** to keep praying – the promises that God has made. Finally there's an **INTITIATIVE** for the people to take to see what God will do.

Get these parts into our praying and it will help so much when we feel all bound up and limited when we want to move on and out in the blessings of God.

1) THE INTENSITY OF HIS PRAYER

"OH that you would rend the heavens and come down." That little word 'OH' is a big emotional word – 'OH that you would . . .' There's something deep going on in Isaiah. He has an intense longing for God and he's struggling to find the words to express it. He can only say 'OH'!

We need to know this. If we are to move heaven we must first be moved ourselves beyond all the power of expression at the state of the church, and moved with unutterable longing for God to step in and do what only He can do.

"Oh, that you would rend the heavens." The heavens are pictured as a curtain which conceals God from our eyes. Isaiah is crying out – "Draw back the curtain. Lift the curtain – please, please *come down* to us and be with us where we are." Already in 63:15, he has appealed to God to *look down* from heaven. But that's not enough. Now he cries out from his heart – "Please *come* down." He feels that the state of the people is such that it's so desperate that it needs some personal manifestation of God's presence which would deal with any opposition.

He visualises how he sees the effects of God coming – *"The mountains would tremble before you!"* And that happened when the Lord descended on Mount Sinai – *"As when fire sets twigs ablaze and causes water to boil."*

The double moral effect of a visitation of God would be that of *fire* – first to burn up the dross of our sin, and then to cause us to burn with love and zeal for Him.

Desire a Visitation

Why should we long for such a visitation? Merely to vindicate ourselves? Just to fill our churches? I hope not. This is why – "Come down to make your name known to your enemies and cause the nations to quake before you!"

This is not a prayer asking to make life more comfortable for ourselves. It's a prayer asking for God to vindicate His character. People had been thinking, "All these troubles we've had, this God stuff doesn't work. God is dead. He counts for nothing." Isaiah is asking, "Lord, show them it's not true!"

He knows that God has done this kind of thing before. *"For when you did awesome things that we did not expect, you came down, and the mountains trembled before you."* God had exceeded all their expectations once before by personally coming down on Mount Sinai and causing the very mountains, let alone the people, to shake at His presence. God did it back then. *"Since ancient times no-one has heard, no ear has perceived, no eye has seen any God besides you, who acts on behalf of those who wait for him."*

Repeated Interventions

Looking back through the history of God's people, it was the Lord's repeated interventions on their behalf which was His distinguishing characteristic. It showed Him up as the living God in contrast to the dead gods of the surrounding nations. Such manifestations of God's power are not given away unconditionally. They are granted as Isaiah knows only too well to those *'who wait for Him.'*

That's the basis upon which God coming and working among us is to be known. Spelling that out, Isaiah says, *"You come to the help of those who gladly do right, who remember your ways."* Do we want to meet God in such a way that He intervenes on our behalf? Do the right things right now! Never forget that the way God works is always along the track of that which is loving, joyful, patient, good, faithful – it's when we obey what we already know God wants from us that puts us in the place where God isn't being grieved or quenched. He will come down to us in some way or other.

But the trouble was that God wasn't meeting Israel back then. Instead of enjoying His presence and experiencing His power, she was bearing the rod of His anger, just as we are today.

So Isaiah faces up to this and his cry for God's *intervention* turns into a personal *involvement*.

2) THE INVOLVEMENT IN HIS PRAYER.

It's never enough to pray, however intense and with fervour we make it, unless we personally get involved. We can't stand off from people saying – "If only *they* were more committed. If only *they* changed." Like Isaiah we must have humility and honesty. As a prophet Isaiah had often needed to stand up in God's name and castigate the people for their sins.

Talking to the people he said, *"You are this"* or – *"You are that."* But coming before God in prayer he climbs down and confesses he's not much better before a holy God – "WE have continued to sin. WE have done wrong." As the old song puts it – *"It's me, it's me, it's me O Lord, Standing in the need of prayer."*

We will get nowhere with God if we try standing aloof criticising others but not acknowledging our own selfishness and indifference to God's ways in in our lives. The church is as she is largely because we are as we are. *"All of us have become like one who is unclean, and all our righteous acts are like filthy rags."* These verses have been used evangelistically but the prophet was speaking of God's people and the pollution which stained even their holiest acts.

Do you know these lines?
"Not for our sins alone
Thy mercy, Lord, we sue;
Let fall Thy pitying glance
On our devotions too—
What we have done for Thee,

And what we think we do."

Isaiah says: "*We all shrivel up like a leaf, and like the wind our sins sweep us away. No-one calls on your name or strives to lay hold of you; for you have hidden your face from us and made us waste away because of our sins."*

Swept Along

Our very bodies bear the marks of our disobedience to God. Just like a leaf, we wither and die and drop to the ground. Then like the wind catching the fallen leaves and blowing them along – we are so easily swept along by wrong. But the most terrible aspect of Israel's sin wasn't so much the impact upon themselves, but its effect upon God. Its causing Him to give up on us to the *consequences* of our sin. It's this Isaiah faces in verse 7: *"No-one calls on your name or strives to lay hold of you."* Generally we don't regard prayerlessness as a very serious matter – but here Isaiah singles it out as the supreme evidence of an abandoned nation, as we shall see. But please notice the very significant terms that Isaiah uses to describe prayer. He describes it as calling on God's Name. It's a work of the heart more than the lips. He describes it as striving to lay hold of God.

Striving to Lay Hold

Taking the promises and by faith we make them our own – it's a very striking phrase – striving or laying hold of God. This teaches us that it's not always easy to gain access to God in prayer. It requires the concentration of all our powers. When we pray for real it takes a lot of energy, a lot of work. A lot of concentration – which is probably our big problem – wandering thoughts!

Half-Hearted Praying

Why were the people so lacking in prayer even when life is really tough for them? You may know the story of the elderly couple facing a crisis. The husband turned to his wife and said, "Well, I guess that we will need to pray about this." And she replied, "Has it come to that!" Why is it only in times of crisis do we really get down to prayer? But here, they aren't even doing that! Isaiah explains: *"For you have hidden your face from us and made us waste away because of our sins."*

They were prayer-less because they had so provoked God by their sin that He had withdrawn His presence – which alone can evoke prayer –

and had literally melted them down into the hand of their iniquities. That is – He had made them helpless to resist the destructive power of their own iniquities, which were driving them from one excess of sin to another. In short, they were an abandoned nation.

So ends Isaiah's confession of their sin with which he identifies himself. "We're all involved in those things that cut us off from your power and presence in our lives." We will truly not get anywhere if we try to stand apart from the state of the Church around us or the state of our nation – "Oh we're better than that. We're better than them."

In Melt-Down

Let's admit that before a HOLY God we're in melt-down. We deserve nothing from His hand. What a picture. Don't you see that it bears a real resemblance to our own day. We say we want God to come down and do things in our midst. We may even get intense in asking Him to come. But we're unfitting for Him, godless, prayerless, helpless – but don't stop there!

Yes we want God to move through our lives and the life of our family and church with power. Pray like Isaiah with INTENSITY and INVOLVEMENT confessing that we fall very short of what we should be. Get specific about it – remember how the New Testament puts it? "If we confess our SINS" – plural – as the Puritans used to say, "Descend to the particular" – face up to specific areas where we fall short of what God wants.

It's not saying, *"I am a sinner Lord and ask for your forgiveness."* But – *"I said this. I did this. I didn't say or do what I should have said and done in this situation."* And here now is the INCENTIVE for striving after God.

3) THE INCENTIVE IN HIS PRAYER.

"Yet, O Lord, you are our Father." Never forget the special relationship we have and thus the responsibility which rests upon a father to take care of his needy children. Earlier in his prayer Isaiah had spoken of God as a *Father* and he comes back to it because that's our incentive for believing God will step in and do good things for us.

Not only is He our *Father,* Isaiah adds this: *"We are the clay, you are the potter."* They were certainly as helpless as the clay to help themselves, and were utterly dependent on God's sovereign intervention to take them out of melt-down and mould them afresh for better things. So, Isaiah has appealed to God as FATHER and as POTTER but he also takes hold of Him as CREATOR – *"We are all the work of your hand."* This is the ground of his appeal for God's mercy – *"Do not be angry beyond measure, O Lord; do not remember our sins for ever. Oh, look upon us we pray, for we are all your people."*

The Father's Heart

What Father's heart could be unmoved by such an appeal? And one last ground of appeal as an incentive to have God coming down to bless is this – the state of the Holy Land itself. These were regarded as HOLY cities but they had become a wilderness or like a desert. *"Jerusalem a desolation. Our holy and glorious temple, where our fathers praised you, has been burned with fire, and all that we treasured lies in ruins."*

Everything that marked a special relationship with God had been destroyed. And we might feel that there's not much left in many of today's churches that seems to show a special relationship to God as His redeemed people – His special people is there?

And after Isaiah has set this pathetic picture before the Lord – He's prayed with INTENSITY – OH LORD we need you to step in – and don't we need the same thing today? He's prayed with INVOLVEMENT – I'm part of the problem not part of the solution. I'm not above the people in need. I draw a circle and step into it and include myself in the need for your mercy.

I think it's not so much the love of God that we need so that our church as well as our lives get back into God's blessing – it's His mercy. As we pray with INTENSITY (not casual words) and pray with INVOLVEMENT (I'm in need not just other people) We pray with an INCENTIVE – Because we know the kind of God that we are praying to – A FATHER, POTTER and CREATOR – we can rely upon Him.

So we can conclude our prayer as Isaiah does looking for an INITIATIVE to be taken by God – *"After all this, O Lord, will you hold yourself back? Will you keep silent and punish us beyond measure?"*

4) THE INITIATIVE IN GOD'S RESPONSE.

And when Isaiah speaks of God holding Himself back the phrase recalls the scene in Genesis 45, when Joseph couldn't hold himself back after he'd listened to Judah's appeal for Benjamin's release – and he wept aloud.

Question! Could the God of Israel hear such an appeal from the lips of Isaiah – and later from the Jews in exile themselves in Babylon – and not be moved to pity? The answer is, no He couldn't. He did rend the heavens and come down to their aid. He did it by miraculously raising up Cyrus, a pagan king, to set His people free, and to charge them to return to Jerusalem and build again the Temple.

God's Action
God *did* come down and restore what they had lost. Let's get this firmly fixed in our minds and hearts. It will work wonders in and through us if we do. It has always been God's distinguishing characteristic – that which shows Him up as the living God – to INTERVENE on behalf of His people when they really recognise their need and truly cry to Him.

Our Need
But my big concern is this – do we recognise the desperateness of our own need right now? Are we really prepared to cry out to Him with INTENSITY right now?

600 years later, in answer to the prayers of a handful who were looking for the consolation of Israel – God did rend the heavens and come down – yes – He came down literally and in person – THE PERSON of our Lord Jesus Christ, at Bethlehem, to deliver not merely a nation from captivity, but the world from spiritual slavery, through His death and resurrection!

A little later still, in answer to the prayers of 120 disciples, He CAME DOWN again and again in the person of the Holy Spirit at Pentecost, to empower His church to live for Him.

And throughout history He has COME DOWN again and again, in answer to the prayers of His people. Not in any new or further visible appearance – that's because JESUS CHRIST is God's last Word to the world, until He appears in judgment – but – He has come down to apply afresh and in divine power the all-inclusive blessings of the Incarnation and of Pentecost to His languishing church.

He has come down in spiritual revival in different parts of the world. He's done it again and again. But OH – how desperately we really need Him to rend the heavens and do it again in our day and in our place and in our lives!

Rend the Heavens

Nothing less than such a visitation of the glory of the Almighty God will meet the needs of the church today. May He give us eyes to see the church as He sees it. May He give us hearts to feel as He feels about it. And may He give us wills to pray as Isaiah prayed until in His mercy and His Sovereign grace once more He rends the heavens and comes down. "OH that you would REND the heavens and come down."

"Now to him who is able to do immeasurably more than all we ask or imagine, according to his power that is at work within us, to him be glory [INSTEAD OF SHAME!] in the church and in Christ Jesus throughout all generations, [INCLUDING OURS!] for ever and ever! Amen."

When He comes down God will fill us with His Holy Spirit. And He wants for us a continuous filling. Let the Holy Spirit come and do God's very best. Let me conclude this chapter by telling you what that means.

First: Constantly yield to the promptings of the Spirit.

There's no unwillingness on God's part in giving us the power and fullness of the Holy Spirit. No – if there are any blockages, if there is any hesitation, if there's any withholding, it's me! So *obey* the promptings of the Spirit. Obey what He reveals of His will for our attitudes and action through His Word. Let the Holy Spirit come down and not only indwell us but fill us because there's no holding back to the Lordship of Christ over our lives.

Second: Let the Holy Spirit who indwells us fill us by constantly appropriating the strength of the Spirit.

Let me tell you something of priceless value if we want God to come down in blessing in and through our lives. I have got to learn to feed on Christ in my heart by faith – and the normal way in which I feed on Christ in my heart (according to the New Testament) is by feeding on God's Word.

I suspect that many Christians are suffering from spiritual malnutrition. It's the cause, I think, of a great deal of our failure, which is otherwise unexplained. I believe it explains a lack of robust spiritual health in many Christian lives. We need to feed on God's Word regularly. To get daily food from God I've got to spend time with my Bible open; mental effort is needed to discover the meaning of the Bible, and to apply it to life. I've got to do much more than just read it. I must try to fix it in my mind.

Now a caution here – If someone expects something wonderful to happen every day in his Bible reading, think again. We will not necessarily have a sense of the immediate presence of God when we open our Bible and read His Word. It's not normal for God to give us an immediate sense of His presence at any time. Nearly always He mediates His Word to us through another channel. It's important to open the Word of God and to believe that God is speaking, though we may feel very tired, very under the weather. We may not feel that it's doing us good. This is vital for God to not only come down to indwell but to fill us and do things through us – we constantly appropriate the strength of the Holy Spirit by letting the Word of God dwell in us richly.

Third: Let the Holy Spirit fill us by constantly sharing the blessings of the Spirit.

Here lies a very simple paradox, understood by every Christian of experience. If I hold in my hand a glass of water, it may seem strange to you if I say that the way to keep this glass full of water is to pour it out. But if you are a Christian I think you'll see this – the way to maintain the fullness of the Holy Spirit, the vitality, the blessing of God is this – pour out what we receive to other people. That's what Jesus said in John 7 – as we drink, rivers of living water will flow from us – and then we will need to drink from Him again.

As we receive the Word of God, we will discover things that are treasures and riches. We will say, "I've never seen that before; I want to pass it on to others" – and very certainly God will give us that opportunity. There will be a friend to share the thought with. There will be someone who needs to hear that. And as we go to tell them of it, we will find that the Holy Spirit is giving us strength.

Summary

Let's just sum this up shall we, because it's all important. Do we feel that we and our church are in some kind of exile – we feel limited and unblessed? We're not free and uninhibited.

The place where things change is as we pray for God to step in and do something by coming down in power to fill us. He indwells us – but with an INTENSITY let's ask for a greater release of His power in and through us.

Thinking Personally
Let's not think this is the need of other people because they are not what they should be. That may be true – but *we* are INVOLVED in need of God's mercies, compassion and care. Let's tell God that.

We have a wonderful INCENTIVE to do so – never ever forget that the God we relate to is our FATHER – He will want to mould us like clay to conform us to the image of Christlikeness. He has the power to do that.

Ask Him to take that INITIATIVE by removing any hindrances – let Him fill us by His Spirit.

Constantly obey. Constantly yield to the promptings of the Spirit. Don't grieve the Holy Spirit – become sensitive. Don't blunder along. Wait for His promptings. Don't starve our soul. Constantly share the blessing of the Spirit. Share the blessing – don't hoard your blessing. Don't you want to live a clean life? Then let the Holy Spirit fill you.

Christian worker, don't you want to make the best and the most of the time that is left to you? Of course you do. Then let the Holy Spirit fill you.

Christian parent, don't you want your home to be the very best it can – a little Christian church, a house of God, a gate of heaven? Then let the Holy Spirit who has come down and indwells you, fill you.

Christian businessman, don't you want your business to show forth the principles in which you believe? Then let the Holy Spirit fill you.

Christian soldier, don't you want to stand against all the wiles of the devil, the hosts of wickedness in heavenly places?

"OH, THAT YOU WOULD REND THE HEAVENS AND COME DOWN."

You've come by the Holy Spirit. But come with all your mighty power unlimited to do in and through me all that you want – TO YOUR GLORY.

(7) ROAD CLOSED

I was travelling home from a church meeting and making good time. Then I came to a detour. The problem was, it was not well marked. I knew where I wanted to go but just couldn't get there. By the time I had made my way round it added three hours to a three hour journey. Have you ever had the same frustration? I'm sure that many of you have. I've learned that over the years it's not just car journeys where I have to face detour signs. This is life!

Facing Detours

Some of you know what it is to face detours. You know where you want to go but just can't get there. You've been dating for years. You are asked to a special meeting at a restaurant. You assume that this will be a proposal. Then he doesn't say, "Will you marry me" but – "I think we need time out."

Listen to this comment that came to me by email - for a couple of years he had been her best friend and she was great fun to be with. Now, at long last, he was about ask a big, big question – *"There are many benefits to being single, but a time comes when one wants a companion to share life with. One who will see the best in me, be supportive, caring and loyal, sharing my happiness and my sorrows."*

He was so pleased to see a knowing gleam come into her eyes. And then she said - "I think it's a wonderful idea! I'll help you choose which puppy to buy." *Another road blocked!*

Some of you know what it is to see road closed signs in marriage. You anticipate children. It's what's next – suddenly you're hit with a road called 'Infertility' – there's no way through. You wonder how long is this detour going to take? Will it last for months or years?

You've lived a long time and faced many losses through death. But now it's different. You didn't want to see this son or daughter die. This is not the order of things – you should go first.

You are in your fifties and you're sitting in your car. You have never been out of work. You've always worked hard. And now you've heard those words – "Sorry, but we have to let you go." You can't believe this but it's happened. How long will I be waiting before I can get back where I want to be?

In the Book of Acts 8 we will see that the early followers of Christ hit road closures and detours. These were difficult times, *"On that day a great persecution broke out against the church at Jerusalem, and all except the apostles were scattered throughout Judea and Samaria."*

This is a major detour. The church in Jerusalem is going places. It's a great time. People anticipate it will keep growing and making a difference for the city. It's exciting. Suddenly there is this brutal attack of persecution. The church is thrown all over the place.

Saul of Tarsus is trying to blow up the church. People are running to any place where they can take cover. I think if you'd asked anyone *before* the detour, "How are things?" I think they would have given glowing reports – "It's fantastic. Great times. Exciting growth curve." The church was growing so fast that they needed to appoint deacons to handle the practical implications.

There was Philip and Stephen – great characters. Philip was so effective in ministry. Later in Acts 21 we see he is married and living in Caesarea on the coast with his family. He has 4 daughters who were all prophets.

Ask Philip, "What was it like before the persecution? Before Saul came and upset things, how was it?" I think he would have said, "It was amazing. The power of God was present. The Holy Spirit was upon us all. People were receiving Christ as Lord. The power of God was on the outside and inside of people freeing them to be their best and God's best. They loved, forgave, served. Miracles were happening. Jesus had transferred His wonder working power into the Apostles – incredible miracles had happened. People who had given themselves to the dark-side were now walking in the light. I'm telling you, it was 3,000 to start things off on the Day of Pentecost but then after that – it just kept multiplying. There were 5,000 – and it wasn't a private faith. They were going public with it. Thousands were baptised. Talk about excitement."

Road Closure

That was before the persecution began. That was before the road closure. Conflict was escalating in Jerusalem. Peter and John were arrested and threatened. Then other believers were persecuted. Stephen was arrested and stoned to death – a horrible way to die. People in the Jerusalem church just ran for their lives.

The people who were living as Christians back then – none of them wanted to end up in Samaria. This was a major detour. Samaritans' hated Jews and Jews hated them. It had been a long time coming.

It was in this region of Galilee up north and Jerusalem to the south - that Jesus did most of His ministry. Very little was done in Samaria. There was such a hatred that had been going on for 900 years. David was king and had a son called Solomon. He was wise but he was morally corrupt and compromised the faith. The people of God were taxed a lot and they drifted morally. After he died the people had a civil war and split – 10 tribes to the North who kept the name Israel. The 2 tribes to the south with the city of Jerusalem were called Judah.

The people in the North stopped travelling down to Jerusalem to worship at the Temple. They built their own worship centres in places like Bethel and Dan. Later they even developed their own temple. When the Assyrians invaded the 10 tribes were overwhelmed. They took them into exile. Some managed to get back to this northern region. The people in Jerusalem hated those who came back, figuring that the gene pool had been contaminated during their time in exile.

The hate continued. There was a time when enemies attacked Jerusalem and the Samaritans did all that they could to support the attackers. The people in Jerusalem never forgot that. If you walked through Samaria as a Jew this was the custom. You would shake out your clothes as you left. In this way you brought nothing contaminated out with you. You shook the dust right out. You didn't go through Samaria if you could help it. It was a straight route but people did detours rather than go through Samaria.

When Saul starts kicking believers out and persecution is arising - people going to Samaria – that's not where they want to be. This is a detour. No-one planned to go there but this is where they are.

Acts 8:5 says something strange: *"Philip went down to a city in Samaria and proclaimed the Christ there."* He ends up in Samaria and decided to do there what he did in Jerusalem. He didn't want to go there but decided to preach Christ there just as he had done in Jerusalem.

"When the crowds heard Philip and saw the miraculous signs he did, they all paid close attention to what he said. With shrieks, evil spirits came out of many, and many paralytics and cripples were healed. So there was great joy in that city" (Acts 8:6).

Some man walks into your town and yells out, "A man was crucified and buried but He's alive again now." You might want to find out if he's insane. And if so, is he harmless? But if that same man also does amazing things like taking a friend of yours who has been blind his whole life and this man sees in the name of the risen Christ. That gets your attention.

Philip began to tell them about Jesus, *"When they believed Philip as he preached the good news of the kingdom of God and the name of Jesus Christ, they were baptised, both men and women."*

This is amazing – the same thing that happened in Jerusalem is now happening in Samaria. It can't be! In Samaria, where no-one wants to go! This is where Philip goes on a detour and Belief is happening. Baptism is happening. People are coming to faith and identifying themselves with the *Jesus Way.*

Word gets back to Jerusalem and the believers are freaked out by this. *"When the apostles in Jerusalem heard that Samaria had accepted the word of God, they sent Peter and John to them."*

This was a couple of their best men sent to check things out. Something is going on up there. Surely there's no way that God would give His Spirit to Samaritans. When Peter and John see what's going on they pray for the believers. They haven't experienced the power of the Holy Spirit.

"Then Peter and John placed their hands on them, and they received the Holy Spirit" (Acts 8:17) This is the power of God IN them. They are now free to live the best of ways. In Samaria we now have the complete work of God just as it had been in Jerusalem.

God in Action

God is at work now in Samaria. This is important to note. Often we view our detours as wasted time. In fact I would guess that the last detour that you went on didn't have you saying, *"Oh great – Let's see what happens now. God has given me this detour so that something wonderful will happen that would not have happened if I'd gone straight to my destination."*

We look at our detours as a huge waste of time and inconvenience. So we waste our detours. When we're on a detour we develop a syndrome called WHEN AND THEN – when we get back on the path we wanted to be on anyway, then we'll start living life again.

When I get through college then.
When I get through this monotonous job and get promoted then.
When we finally have the baby then.
When I do get married then.
When we get out of this house into a dream house then.

We think when we're somewhere else then we'll start to live. But life is happening right now. Opportunities are now. We can waste our life because we think that the detours don't count. That's not what we see with Philip. The detours count. Samaria isn't Philip's plan. He didn't want to go there. Since he is there he simply says, *"I will keep living for Christ. While this terrible thing has happened I will keep living the Jesus way."* Never ever let your detour be wasted. You wouldn't have chosen it and didn't ask for it but don't waste it.

So the girl with the boyfriend who wants time out – suddenly has time she didn't have before. She didn't want or expect it. The road closed sign went up and she must choose what to do. And what she chooses will make all the difference. All the difference! Whether she will take the free time and invest it wisely.

Redeem the Time
What do you do to redeem the time when your life is detoured? And it happens to all of us. Sometimes when the detours come it's when we need God the most.

Someone was telling me that he grew up in a family that was really as good as you can get. There was nothing to change for the better. The family went to church and were secure in all areas of their life. Sometimes parents will say, "We won't make church a priority for our kids." They don't say that of football practice or lots of other things that just aren't as important. In church we learn of the essentials of eternity. The kid says, "I don't want to go this week." That's okay we'll stop! You can't quit football but you can church. What are you thinking? All kids will go through times like that. This man was saying he went to church and had heard all about Jesus. He gave his life to Christ and knew His power. He was 17, his sister had just gone off to university. His younger brother was 12 – It was then that he discovered that his father was having an affair with his secretary. No one knew but him and his mother. They talked together about not talking about it. They hoped and prayed for a repentance.

A real 180 degree change! They prayed on their own and together. When the young man prayed at this difficult time he said he needed God more than anything. Over the next months his father moved out of the house and then back. Mum would forgive and he would come home 13 times! There was remorse and then he would feel a pull and leave again. He saw his mother on her knees clinging to his dad begging him not to go. And he would leave.

He was 19 and strong. Remember the power you had at 19? Watching his dad walk out he said he decided in a rage he is not going to leave again. He went after his father. He hit the door and was bounced back. He ran for the door again and bounced back. There was nothing in the door. He hit that open space again but he hit an invisible barrier again. He said I remember sinking down. He said, I believe that God stopped me and saved my life and my dad. I don't know how that happens but it did. He needed God to help him through. He was dating the young woman he was to later marry. He was sitting next to his future mother-in-law. He knew that he was loved by them. She touched his hand and said, "We know." In that moment he knew it was now public knowledge. It broke him. He wept and wept and she just held him.

There are times we end up in a place we don't want to be. At times it's because of what we have done. Often it's because of what other people do that touches upon us. It closes the road ahead.

Saul blew up the church in Jerusalem. Something blows up your family or your job. At times like this you have to ask God for help. Have you noticed that on the detours there's often a vulnerability? Things are not as you want so you have to get serious, "God please help me. I don't know how to help myself or the people around me." This man said, *"I knew what God had called me to do before my family was wrecked. This mission has not changed. It is to love God with all I've got."*

Unchanged Mission
Circumstances change but a mission doesn't change. So, like Philip stay true to the mission. He didn't want to be in Samaria but he stayed true to the mission. And God used Philip in a powerful way. God started to do amazing things in Samaria as He had in Jerusalem. Among other things Philip finds himself on another detour. The Spirit sends him to another road on the way to Africa. A man in a chariot goes by reading from a scroll. He is a financial leader for the Queen of present day Sudan. He has a spiritual hunger. He has a valuable 700 year old scroll. Philip hears him reading from Isaiah and helps him understand the good news of the gospel. The man got it and was baptised. It was amazing – 3,000 then 5,000 in Jerusalem. Then Samaria with great crowds and now for one man!

We may be on a detour. God has a reason for allowing this detour into our life. The reason may not be *you!* Philip was on a detour because of Saul's persecution and the gospel comes to a Samaritan. Then to one man on his way to Africa and who knows the impact now. Could it be that God allows the detours in our life not so much for us but for someone else?

You are in a hospital waiting room. You don't want to be there and it's breaking your heart. It's a detour. Could it be that God has one person there who needs to hear about Christ or might need prayer? Could it be that you were on the career ladder and then it's road closed and no job? Could it be that God has another place for you to help another person?

My mission doesn't change just because my circumstances change. May be even on the detour it's not about me but someone else. It's tragic if we put our lives into neutral because of the detour. This is wasted time and we want to get back to where we want to be.

Great Things
God does great things in the detours. We expect to see God in the main events of our lives not the detours. We expect to see God in the face of a new baby. We don't expect to see God in infertility. We expect to meet God when we move into our dream house not when we move out of it unemployed and into a small rented house. We expect to meet God when we're employed not unemployed. We don't want the detours. God is just as active when you get side-tracked.

Psalm 46 verse 1: "God is our refuge and our strength, an ever present help..." – *when?* - when we need God because we're in trouble.

David's Detours

Did you know that King David spent a decade of his life on a detour? David who killed Goliath. David who was all up-and-coming in the eyes of the people – King Saul became jealous and for a decade he lived like a dog in the desert wilderness. Saul was out to kill him. Out of that detour David gained a trust in God.

He wrote Psalms during this time. *"The Lord is my shepherd, I shall not be in want. . . Surely goodness and love will follow me all the days of my life, and I will dwell in the house of the Lord for ever."* During that nasty detour forced on David he sings of not living in fear, because God is with him.

Know This

In your financial implosion know this – HE IS WITH YOU.
When you have to wait, and wait and wait – HE IS WITH YOU.
In the terrible conflict – HE IS WITH YOU.
In the midst of betrayal – HE IS WITH YOU.
When your parents are divorcing – HE IS WITH YOU.
When your marriage is falling apart – HE IS WITH YOU.

When you want to live in Jerusalem but find yourself in Samaria where you don't want to be – HE IS WITH YOU. He is always with you – so wait on God in the detours of your life. Expect His presence and power and His love – because *HE* is with you.

An Energy Drain

There's a false idea which drains us of energy when faced with detours. It's that we can finally get things sorted and settled down. We strive to solve all the problems we face, work through all the challenges, and resolve all the conflicts in our relationships. Our energies are invested to finish up projects and meet deadlines in the vain hope that then we can sit back comfortably.

There's a great emphasis in our day to get the right job, save enough money, accumulate the security of a home and comfortable surroundings, establish the right friendships, and travel to see the places we've always wanted to visit. Also, we are pressed on by the illusion that if we can just get through the pressures we are presently facing, then we can relax. The problem is that our preconceived ideas of what settled security is going to be are in themselves detours which may be keeping us from God's best for our lives.

The question I am forced to ask myself is, *"Where will I be when I arrive at where I am going? What will I have accomplished when I think I have accomplished my goal?"* When I begin to review those destinations with the Lord, I'm usually discomfited by the realisation that He has plans which are way beyond my own.

My experience is that the Lord constantly allows those disturbances which will wake us out of cosiness. He will use problems and conflicts to get us moving again. Whenever life falls apart in some area, he is giving us a chance to grow. Life really becomes exciting when we accept, rather than resist, the rough, tight places that wake us up to new ways of being our best for Him. Every event which befalls us has a meaning beyond itself. Our task is to ask the Lord what He's trying to say to us.

Back from the Detour

How can I get back from a detour? That's not really the question, after all. The real question is: Have we asked the Lord what is the next step of His strategy for us in the adventure of growing in our relationship with Him? Am I becoming the person He meant me to be, and doing the particular thing I was born to accomplish? If that is clear, what is the first step to be taken today?

(8) DARK DAYS

"Here are some things that children should be learning in school, but they aren't. Not all of these lessons have to do with academics. Here are some basic rules that may not have found their way into the standard curriculum.

Some (perhaps all) of these should be credited to Charles Sykes, author of '*Dumbing Down Our Kids*'

Rule 1: LIFE IS NOT FAIR.
Get used to it.

Rule 2: THE WORLD WON'T CARE ABOUT YOUR SELF-ESTEEM.
It will expect you to accomplish something before you feel good about yourself.

There are plenty more like that! Pastor Alan Smith makes this comment in an email devotional –

I think there are some good points to be learned by students in this material. The message I see repeated throughout is "don't expect for life to be easy." Interestingly enough, that's one of the messages that Jesus left with his disciples. Life for a Christian will not always be easy. At times, it will be very difficult. And sometimes it helps just to know that in advance.

As the apostle Peter said: "Do not think it strange concerning the fiery trial which is to try you, as though some strange thing happened to you; but rejoice to the extent that you partake of Christ's sufferings, that when His glory is revealed, you may also be glad with exceeding joy."

The important insight for us is to know this - life isn't ever going to be easy in this fallen and broken world, but God promises to resource us with strength and power to help us get through. However, here is the rub – IS THAT ALWAYS TRUE?

Here's the big question. It's one we will ask at some time in our lives: "Does the Maker of the stars hear the sound of my breaking heart?"

People we care about cry out to God and the response appears to be silence or "No". We wonder where is God in this? We have a family or work situation that takes us into trauma.

David wrote a song about this that you'll probably know. In Psalm 23 he writes about the shadow of death. The Hebrew really means the *darkest* time of your life. The hardest thing you have ever been through. And that was King David – he knew times like this.

A lot of people would prefer to avoid the valley and jump to the next mountain but it doesn't happen. Sometimes we do all sorts of ridiculous things to stop facing up to the fact that we are in a valley.

Maybe the dark place you are in right now is the right place for you. Maybe that is going to get you closer to God. I know that will be hard to accept when in the valley.

We always think the great times will be the mountain experiences when we get the job, get the good marriage, have a nice family. But we don't live on the mountain top all the time. We do find ourselves in the valley.

When people walk into a church service they come in with pain, problems, pressures – it's life! We need the courage to face it and handle it well.

It Happens

I listened to this story. A young man was out serving Christ and seeing a lot of blessing. His wife has a baby that is still-born. After crying with her in the hospital room he went to his car and sat there for a long time with just one word he was yelling, "Why God, why? Can't you save a little baby?" He was so angry and bitter. After this he couldn't talk to God at all. He didn't want to go back to church. "I would be faking it" he said.

Another father lost his young daughter. Someone said to him, "Don't stop believing in God." He replied, "Don't worry about me. I won't stop believing in God. I just hate Him that's all!"

Some of you may be feeling this. Sometimes we just lack the courage to say it because we can't say something like that, can we?

This was the 'valley' for these people. What they didn't realise was that God was *with* them in their valley. We need to see that from Scripture to get the help we need for such dark times.

There are Bible passages we can quote where the impression is given that if we live for God all will work out well for us. We will be answered by God even before we call. And yet there are times when you may cry out to God and you feel God is turning away from you. We feel God-forsaken rather than God blessed. Job knew this – trying to find God in his suffering and not finding Him.

At the funeral for a little baby who died after taking a few breaths. The funeral director tried to be comforting by saying to the dad, *"Well at least he died as a baby and you didn't know him yet."* He thought to himself – *"But that's my problem* – I didn't know him and I wanted to know him. I will never watch him grow up. I will never teach him how to ride a bike. That's my problem. God why did you take him from me?" He said to his wife, "I love you and I'll always be here for you. But I don't know if I will ever smile again."

There's a modern song that captures this mood –
What can I do to make you smile again,
Just smile again.
I'd like to know what's on your mind
Because I see you crying all the time
I don't understand
Who'd want to hurt your heart like this and
Cause you so much pain

That's the problem! It seems to us that God does!

The song goes on to say --
Here's my shoulder
You can lean on me
I want to see you happy

But where is God at such dark times? He doesn't seem to care! Why does God say NO?

I had a series of emails from a mum and dad – Their son is in his early twenties. He had dedicated himself to the service of Christ and this had taken him abroad. His dad needed to fly to get him home as he had experienced a really bad nervous breakdown. *But he only wanted to serve Christ!* That stuff happens a lot. For every healing by Christ's power in my experience there are those who don't get healed. Is it us? Are we not close enough to God?

In John 11 Mary and Martha have sent a message to Jesus saying: *"Lord, the one you love is sick. Your good friend."* Do you know what Jesus did? He stayed away until four days after he had died. Coming back He could prove that He is the resurrection and the life.

Isn't that all we ask for? Sometimes God says YES, at other times he says NO.

"And God it's when you say NO that I hit trouble. I don't get it. I don't understand why. Why is it that someone who has loved and served Christ all their life is just coming to retirement age and they end up with multiple tumours in their body and they die in pain? Why, God, when they have served you and love you?"

You end up praying, *"Lord, take this person please, please. Why are they still alive, it won't get any better? They're not comfortable. They're in pain. The morphine isn't helping a lot. Take this person please."*

Unanswered Questions

Why does this person live? Why, God? When God says *'no'* what do you do with that? Doesn't the Bible say that Jesus Christ is the same today as He was in the past? Didn't Jesus tell us to be like a bold neighbour knocking and knocking for a response and help? He tells us to keep on knocking and keep on asking to get what we ask for. Jesus said that we are to be like the widow who goes to an unjust Judge and because she keeps asking she gets justice. God isn't unjust so how much more should we get from Him.

Keep asking and praying. How do I understand it then when God says 'No'? Some deaths are clean deaths. You live 90 years and die in your sleep. Some deaths are dirty deaths. If I was to die right now I would think of it as a full life. I've been married to a great wife with a great family. If I went in my sleep it would be a clean death. But what about all those dirty deaths? Those deaths that raise clouds of dust into the eyes of faith.

I've seen so many people like this with the dust of doubt in their eyes. What do you say to them? We grope for answers – but these are some reasons why God says 'No.' This is for you!

Requests

Sometimes our request is wrong. Have we got that? What does it say in James? We pray and don't receive because we ask with the wrong motives. Take a note of that – "God, I want to get married because I'm lonely." That's not a good enough reason. Don't get married until you really know it is the right person. You need to marry a person in it for the long run and they need that from you.

The disciples are often the 'poster people' for those who make wrong requests. They are on top of a mountain with Jesus. Suddenly Moses and Elijah turn up – that's cool! And Jesus dazzles in white – a bright light like a light shining through a sheet – that's what is happening.

They see the deity of Christ shining through Him. They want this experience to last – and the request is denied. There is a boy at the bottom of this mountain who needs to be healed. There are lives to be changed at the bottom of this mountain.

When the disciples find that there are villages where Jesus will not be welcomed they say that He should burn them up! Torch them! And Jesus says REQUEST DENIED! 'I didn't come to torch people I came to transform people."

Remember when James and John put in a request for being the closest to Jesus in His kingdom? What does Jesus say, "No!" He was often saying no to the disciples. The request was wrong.

As the Psalmist said, if we regard iniquity in our heart we shouldn't expect to get our prayers answered. Why would God do that? We don't honour Him. He still loves us and retains the inclination to want to answer our requests immediately – He wants to pour blessings on us, but not if we sin.

And what is SIN? It's an archery term in the Greek language. It simply means we are missing the mark. God's will is to stay true to people and centred on Him through His Word. When we aim for that, God will open a window in heaven. God still loves us but we won't get the blessing.

Sometimes our request is wrong.
Sometimes we are in the wrong.

A Test

Here's another thing, maybe this is a test. I know there is truth in this. But I don't want to stay with this in the wrong way. God isn't testing us to find what we're made of. God knows what we're made of.

Sometimes we have to go through the valley just to get character. Here is where we get depth. This is where we start growing up. I know this but this is what I want to say – at times the pain is too much! Sometimes our faith isn't strengthened by fire, it's melted by fire. Any reader known that?

Sometimes it's too much – "Enough, God, let up." Visit Auschwitz and you will see how maybe 20% were resolute but many became like animals. It was just too much!

Many times it's not your fault. People may say that God says NO because you're paying for your sins – it's not always the case. Actually I get sick and tired of people saying, "The reason you're going through the valley of shadows is because you're just not a good enough Christian. You must have un-confessed sin in your life. You're walking away from God." That may be the case but often it's not true. It bothers me. This is not who God is.

If we want to find out where God is, look at the person with the humble and broken spirit – that's where He lives. *"The Lord is close to the broken-hearted and saves those who are crushed in spirit."* (Psalm 34:18). That's where God is. That's where He lives.

I'm not surprised that Shadrach, Meshach and Abednego found the Lord in the fiery furnace. I'm not surprised that Lazarus found Jesus in the cemetery. That's where He lives. He is always close to the broken-hearted.

Not a Detour

Maybe the detour isn't a detour. Maybe this is where we are supposed to be. Not forever – "Though I walk through the valley" – *through* – we don't build our lives there but we go *through* the valley, we don't jump over it.

This is where we come to find how much He loves us. He comes to the broken-hearted. Jesus said that this is what He would do. We will never know Him closer than when we suffer. We may not *feel* it but it's still true. That's where He is. We cry out – "What a waste!" when a young mother dies of cancer. It does hurt us. But it's not a waste is it? Death is a means of getting more of Christ. There is something *better.* Don't take that away from the sufferer.

Doubting God
Walk through the valley with your friends and family. However, I need to add this because it's so important – at times of loss and uncertainty we may *doubt* God.

Doubt is not the same thing as unbelief. Doubt is a state of mind in suspension between faith and unbelief. This distinction is vital, because it means we are allowed to have doubts. The Bible makes a clear distinction between *doubt* and *unbelief.* The word 'unbelief' is usually used of a wilful refusal of God. A deliberate rebellion against Him.

The true relationship of *faith and doubt* is closer to that of *courage and fear. Fear* is not the opposite of *courage: cowardice* is.

Fear, in fact, need be no final threat to courage. What courage can't afford is *recklessness.* It takes courage to be a mountain climber but it's courage with careful calculating. It's the same with 'Faith and Doubt.' *Doubt* is not the opposite of faith, *unbelief* is.

Don't be too *hard* on doubt. Please understand that you are allowed to have doubts. Most of us think the people around us are incredibly strong believers; if only you knew! Their motto is: *"If you've got it flaunt it, if you haven't, fake it."*

You come to worship and see the people sitting listening and think they have life sorted – I doubt that! You are allowed to say: "I don't understand." Admitting to doubt doesn't mean you are insulting God.

Curing Doubt
Let me list the *CURES FOR DOUBT:* people have found these helpful.

1) STOP AND THINK.

What is the first thing you do when you've lost something? You think – where was I? Where have I been? *Ask:* "What is the root of the doubt? What is the cause?" Try to unravel the cause. Jude taught: "Be merciful to those who doubt." Some people are not so responsible for their doubts and need *comfort*. Other people are more culpable and need *confronting.*

2) REVIEW THE PLAN OF SALVATION.

Have you ever had a *button* left over when you dressed? You started out wrong and need to start again. You have *doubts?* Go back and ask: "Do I understand the gospel? Am I expecting heaven now and never to come to a place where God will wipe away the tears" – but I have to have the tears for Him to wipe them away! Often the problem is not in the *belief* but the *believer*. Not in the *insufficiency* of truth but in the *self-sufficiency* of the one who trusts. Keeping alive a grateful memory is an art we must grow in. Keep some record of what God has done in our past. Just looking at the Cross alone is enough to know that He does love us. He has dealt with the big eternal issues in our lives – we can trust Him with the small stuff – it's small by comparison!

3) LEARN TO DOUBT YOUR DOUBTS.

This is a skill we can muster over time. Say: "What if I'm wrong to doubt? What if God really does love me?" Turn the whole thing *upside down:* doubting your doubts is very important. It will show you how absurd it can be and blown out of proportion.

In the Enid Blyton Version of Pilgrims Progress - Pilgrim is travelling to the Heavenly City. It's night and dragons are breathing on either side of him. But then he sees that they are chained. Learn to recognise our doubts are chained. There is a reason for the hope that we have.

4) BUILD GOOD FOUNDATIONS.

I have seen too many people drift away. They know *what* they believe but they don't know *why* they believed, so when a problem came and shook them there was no foundation to their faith. Christianity is not true because it *works:* it works because it's *true.* A person can become a Christian for all sorts of reason but – good foundations are vital.

Christian faith is not a leap in the dark – it has a rational basis.

Don't misunderstand Christ's rebuke of Thomas: "Because you have seen me, you have believed; blessed are those who have not seen and yet have believed." Certainly Thomas was rebuked but the question is *WHY.* He was not rebuked because he refused to believe without enough reasons, but because he refused to believe with *MORE* than enough reasons.

For *three years* he had been with *Jesus*. It was unnecessary to ask for the kind of proofs he did. Even with this Jesus didn't demand a *'leap of faith'.* He told Thomas to touch and see. We don't know whether he did.

Life Law
Let me give you a law of life: "Genuine *understanding* generates genuine *faith* and genuine *faith* in turn generates *experience."* Without genuine faith, *experience* is counterfeited by *emotionalism*.

When the women told the disciples: "Jesus is risen" they thought it was incredible. *PETER* got up and ran to the tomb seeking to ascertain the truth of the matter. *FAITH* does not feed on thin air but on *FACTS*. Its instinct is to root itself in *TRUTH,* to earth itself in *REALITY.*

I watched a TV documentary where nervous people were being helped to fly as passengers by an airline. The way they were helped was by being given a lot of information and then carefully testing it out. It's the same when we are struggling in the dark. Go for what we know of God and His ways.

5) ASK FOR PRAYER.

Don't be frightened or too proud to ask for prayer. It's helpful. Don't share it with the *church gossip* but find the kind of people who will come alongside you.

Bible pictures for faith are active and energetic – The ATHLETE, BOXER, SOLDIER. Let's allow someone to be a coach or trainer in our race, fight or battle.

6) BE PRACTICAL.

Interestingly when *Elijah* went through a depression, God did not prescribe a refresher course in Theology. He helped him with food and rest. He gave Him good theology in the context of this.

We can be plagued with doubts because we are dog-tired and need some sleep. Some people are affected by the weather or some anniversary dates. Start forming good habits by talking to yourself about what you know of God despite the darkness.

THESE ARE THE SIX WAYS TO DEAL WITH DOUBTS.

Bring your doubts to God now. Yes, you feel in the dark. Yes, it seems you are in the valley, but look, if you will *not* put your faith in Him what alternative have you? Listen to these words from someone who knows what it's like to be in dark places and valley experiences, "Cast all your anxiety on Him because He cares for you."

(9) FINAL WORDS

In this chapter we're looking at some of the last things a man called Joshua had to say to the people he led into the Promised Land. By now he's an old man. He's wanting to communicate truth in such a way it both challenges and gives a lasting direction to the people of God. What he has to say will help them not to waste their lives. It can do the same for us (Joshua 23:1-16). There are things here worth knowing. They will help us live a Christian life at a more productive level.

I like the question, "How old would you be if you didn't know how old you are?" There is no choice in growing *old*. There is in growing *up.*

A young man, who was also an avid golfer, found himself with a few hours to spare one afternoon. He figured that if he hurried and played very fast, he could get in nine holes before he had to head home. Just as he was about to tee off, an old gentleman shuffled onto the tee and asked if he could accompany the young man as he was golfing alone. Not being able to say no, he allowed the old man to join him. To his surprise, the old man played fairly quickly. He didn't hit the ball far, but plodded along consistently and didn't waste much time. Finally, they reached the ninth fairway and the young man found himself with a tough shot. There was a large pine tree right in front of his ball and directly between his ball and the green. After several minutes of debating how to hit the shot, the old man finally said, "You know, when I was your age, I'd hit the ball right over that tree." With that challenge placed before him, the youngster swung hard, hit the ball up, right smack into the top of the tree trunk and it thudded back on the ground not a foot from where it had originally laid. The old man offered one more comment, "Of course, when I was your age, that pine tree was only three feet tall." You can tell when you are growing old. Children study in history what you studied in current events.

You and I are getting older – but are we growing up? We live in a youth-orientated culture. The older we get the more invisible we may become in society. But while we are still breathing there is something to be and things to do.

Joshua knew the truth of that. Coming to chapter 23, a long time had passed since he led the nation into the Promised Land. They had found rest from their enemies. Old and well advanced in years, Joshua comes out of 'retirement' with a final message for the nation. So – he put on blue jeans, dyed his hair and tried to look 'with-it'? No, it doesn't say that. "I am old and well advanced in years" he says.

Whatever Our Age

It's good to be young, but it's not bad to be old. I remember looking in the mirror as a young preacher and wishing I was older. I thought people would listen to me much more if I was older. Now I look in the mirror and think, 'Who is that old man staring back at me.' Someone said to me, "I'm a young man in an old man's body and I don't like it." I understand that. Everyone wants to live a long life but no-one wants to grow old. Honesty admits that age has its limitations. We may forget things – "Was I going upstairs or downstairs?" "Your face is familiar." "It should be, I've been married to you these past fifty years!"

Getting up in the morning you put your windows on, choppers in, turn up your ears and lean on your walking frame. At night you reverse it. There's more by the bed than in the bed!

Age has its drawback but it can be a gift of God. C.S.Lewis was a great thinker and writer. He died the same day as American President Kennedy and therefore it didn't become as newsworthy as it would have been. The nurse who cared for him said that he was a fighter but the best patient, because he dealt with old age in such a good way.

C.S. Lewis wrote a series of letters to an American lady whom he gave the fictional name of Mary. Just think about the insight that pours from his pen in some of his comments –

"Dear Mary,

Pain is terrible but surely you need not have fear as well. Can you not see death as the friend and deliverer? It means stripping off the body which is tormenting you like taking off a hair shirt or getting out of a dungeon.

What is there to be afraid of? You have long attempted a Christian life. Your sins are confessed and absolved. Has this world been so kind to you that you leave it with such regret? There are better things ahead than any we have behind.

Remember, though we struggle against things because we are afraid of them, it is often the reason we are afraid of them.

Are you struggling and resisting? Don't you think our Lord says to you, 'Peace child, peace, relax, let go. Underneath are the Everlasting Arms. Let go, I will catch you. Do you trust me so little?'

Of course, this may not be the end. Then make it a good rehearsal. Yours, and like you – a tired traveller near the journey's end."

Growing old gracefully!
We can be a bitter old person or we can be a gift. No-one grows old, we are old when we stop growing. A Church Minister when 103 years old was interviewed by a local newspaper reporter. He was asked, "What is it that you have to do to live so long?" He replied, "Don't die!" But a lot of people do die before a final breath leaves their body.

Young people need your experience. Rightly handled, these older years may be the most productive of your life. Joshua the soldier had given way to Joshua the administrator, and now Joshua the advisor. It was less exhausting service and one more suited to his advancing years. I like Joshua when he is a young man. But I appreciate the wisdom of his years.

If we knew we are going to die soon, what would we tell people? Listen to what Joshua had to say. There are great insights here that can greatly help us.

1) GOD IS SOVEREIGN.

An old person acquires memories. Indeed, it's often a sign of advancing years that we say things like, "I remember when" or, "I remember this or that." And it's good to remember – just as long as we remember we may have told that story a dozen times already!

Joshua looks back and says, *"You yourselves have seen everything the Lord your God has done to all these nations for your sake."*

Remember the kind of God He is! *"He fought for you and allotted all the land."* God Himself drove and pushed them out. They had become a cancerous growth in the land that needed to go. God promised the land as an inheritance and they were able to take possession. And we can live by the fact that nothing happens outside the Hand of God. If God is not Sovereign, God is not God. This means I don't have to battle thinking, "It all depends on me."

Annie Johnson Flint once said:
"Christ has no hands but our hands to do His work today.
He has no feet but our feet to lead men in His way.
He has no tongues but our tongues to tell men how He died.
He has no help but our help to bring them to His side."

Annie Johnson Flint was a godly person -- but those words may be misleading. Everything does not depend upon us, and the sooner we realise it the better it will be for us.

Good News, Bad News
This is the good news: God is important. This sounds like bad news: we are not important. We could die tomorrow and in one hundred years' time nobody will think about us. But if that sounds like bad news it only seems it. Because this also means that we can't mess up so badly. Because in the long run it's not that important. We don't have to be God and it reduces the pressure considerably. If we left tomorrow few people would care and the world would go on – that can be taken as a relief!

Do you know that the Book of Joshua begins with one funeral and ends with three? The death of Moses is recorded in chapter 1. The last chapter records the death of Joshua, the death of Joseph (which had happened some three hundred and fifty years earlier – he wanted his bones buried in the Promised Land and they remembered). And there's also the death of the Priest Eleazer. They were giants of the faith, but now they are gone. The world will go on without me. Once I take that to heart it can save me from unnecessary tension.

God is in Charge
Because God is in charge I am responsible to Him. That's not a bad deal. If God is in charge I don't have to worry about His will. Oh what a waste of time it is worrying about whether we are in the will of God or not.

When I'm asked questions about God's will I often ask a couple of questions. "Are you violating the known will of God right now?" And, "If you know what God's will was would you be willing to do it?" If the answer is correct for both we have no worries. God's will is going to find us! God is perfectly capable of working His will out where He finds a willing heart.

Because God is in charge we are free from vested interests. I worry more about my car than I do my neighbours. Ownership implies responsibility. There is a vested interest in what belongs to us. When I realise I don't belong to myself anymore but to God it helps me to relax.

Because God is in charge I am free from trying to run my world by myself. What do I know about this great big God? That He is a Sovereign God of grace! We talk about God's Sovereign Grace but we need to experience it! We've got to experience emotionally the staggering truth that we can't earn our way into God's will for our lives. We can't earn our way into His good books.

Salvation comes to us as a gift from His Sovereign Hand – just as the Promised Land was a gift to His people back in Joshua's time. There's nothing we can do to make ourselves feel like we're really worthy of God. It's first and finally God's gift to us through faith. Only as we believe that God sees us as worthy already, and then accept what He has given us, can we learn to live out of His measure of life rather than that of the people around us or anyone else. God in His Sovereignty does things for me that make me right with Him. That directs my way.

I am okay because God finds me to be okay. When I'm unable to be as useful to Him as I once was – He still finds me to be okay. And when I know that I'm okay because of His Sovereign Grace toward me and not what I do – I never worry again about what other people think of me in the same way. I can even make mistakes. Our performance orientated culture says it's wrong to ever be wrong. But we don't have to be right. We don't have to win all the time. We can actually get things wrong some of the time and it's okay.

A man told me of a friend who used to call him on the telephone on Monday mornings. He would pick up the phone and hear his friend in a deep voice saying – *"Hello, this is God. I have a gift for you today. I want to give you the gift of failing. Today you do not have to succeed. I grant that to you."* Then he would hang up. The man said – *"I would sit there for ten minutes staring at the wall. The first time I couldn't believe it. It was really the gospel. God's love means it's even okay to fail. You don't have to be the greatest thing in the world. You can just be you. And that's okay. In God's name it's okay."*

When we relax into His sovereignty over our lives and tell Him we're acknowledging Him in all of our ways something happens. A marvellous liberation comes over us. We are able to enjoy a Promised Land experience. We can leave behind a fantasising world, we maintain in our head.

No Make-Belief Universe

God doesn't live in a make-believe universe. This is why we miss Him so often. We look for Him in an idealised world and go right past Him in everyday life. God lives with the worst and best of us, but always it's with the real us. That's where God is, and that's why we can miss Him so much. We look for Him in the idealised world, but we go right past Him here in the real world.

Richard Nash wrote a dialogue in 'The Rainmaker' that grasps this idea. It's a secular writing but it gets a big point across. There's a character with the name Starbuck. He's a dreamer and his dreams never really happen for him. He complains about this to Liz – and she knows how to live in reality. After telling her that nothing in his hands is as it is in his head and asking why that's the case she replies that she has no idea but "Maybe it's because you don't have time to see it. You always have to run, to come, to go, maybe it helps you keep company with the world?" Starbuck then says, "You think I'd learn to love it?" Liz replies by talking about her dad. He's ordinary, middle-aged and not very interesting - but at times she watches him more closely and she sees things she'd never seen before. And she says, *"Suddenly, I know who he is and I love him so much I could cry. And I want to thank God I took time to see him real."*

Many of us are forever running trying to find life somewhere. And all the time that life is right here in the Sovereign Lord who comes to live in us to do things through us. It's never enough to know that in theory. We need to let that truth really grip us.

Why not wipe out some time to let this truth take hold? Let it saturate us. Let's reckon on who He is and what He wants to be about in His *sovereign* power, presence and grace in our lives.

Start by deciding to do nothing but reflect and thank Him that He is who He is. Powerful, pardoning and purposeful in our lives. Not at a distance but within us.

Good Dreams

Because God is in charge I can dream. A young woman woke up one morning and told her husband, "I just dreamed that you gave me a pearl necklace. What do you think it means?" "You'll know tonight," he said. That evening the man came home with a small package and gave it to his wife. Delighted, she opened it, only to find a book entitled *"The Meaning of Dreams."* I'm not meaning THAT kind of dream – *a hope-so, wishful-thinking* kind of dream.

Someone has said, *"To fight and lose for a noble cause is better than to fight and win for an ignoble cause."* That sounds good but it isn't true. Surely it's better not to fight at all if you can't win! But God has made sure that no fight for His cause will ultimately fail. The cause we stand for will never die. He will keep His promises. We don't have to play it safe because we already are safe.

The future is ours because the future is His! Joshua is saying what we need to remember - GOD IS SOVEREIGN. Joshua has more to say.

2) PEOPLE ARE SIGNIFICANT.

Joshua wasn't important but he was significant – and it's not the same. We are not important because everything that God wants to happen will happen. We are significant because we are paid for with the blood of Christ. And God allows us to be significant in so far as we co-operate with what He is doing.

So Joshua goes on to say in chapter 1 verse 7, "Be very strong; be careful to obey all that is written in the Book of the Law of Moses, without turning aside to the right or to the left."

We are not significant because we are talented but because we belong to God. As Joshua says, "Hold fast to the Lord your God." The world is always telling us that we give people a bad self-image because we keep talking about sin. That's not true! Let me tell you how to get a poor self-image. Tell yourself you're an expert pilot when you're not and go and try to fly a plane. Tell yourself you're a great builder when you're not and go and build an extension to your house. Tell yourself you're a great singer – again when you're not – and go and hire a concert hall for your performance. All that will give you a bad self-image. Why? Because you're lying to yourself. When we start looking at ourself as we really are that's the beginning of a good self-image. Our significance is not in what we do but what we are.

We are a person that Christ died for and valued so much He wants to share a whole new earth and new heaven with us. That really helps my self-image! And we are a person that Christ by His Spirit comes to indwell and equip for His service. That also helps my self-image a lot! Trying to build self-esteem on any other basis than this is a trivial pursuit.

Joshua could have gone off and retired. But he was concerned for people. And we must always maintain that concern. What can I do to help this person or that person? There is a circle of people we meet regularly – how can I be what God wants me to be to them? How can I help them to get closer to God and ready for eternity?

A tombstone gave this challenge:
"That which I spent that I had.
That which I gave that I have.
That which I left that I lose."

There are givers and takers. The takers often end up bitter. The givers may not have a big bank account but they sleep well at night. We can look out for ourselves – but an old man called Joshua is here to tell us that's not the way to go.

GOD IS SOVEREIGN.
PEOPLE ARE SIGNIFICANT.
Joshua adds to this a crucial factor –

3) COMPROMISE IS SERIOUS.

Notice when Joshua names sins he doesn't mention stealing or adultery – wrong though that is. He talks about compromise. *"If you turn away and ally yourselves with the survivors of these nations that remain among you."*

Intermarrying with these people would mean that the pull away from God would be very strong. Don't put your hand in the fire and pray that it doesn't get burnt. These are among the 'snares and traps for you.' Or, as Joshua vividly paints in his word picture: *"Whips on your backs and thorns in your eyes, until you perish from this good land, which the Lord your God has given you."*

Do you know what they think sunk the Titanic? Not the iceberg. It hit the iceberg. There were small perforations of the hull. Here's what did it for the Titanic. They've discovered that the rivets of the hull were made of below-grade iron so that once water began coming into those compartments and the pressure began to build, the rivets just began to pop apart, one after the other and the compartments opened up wide and that's what sunk the Titanic. Compromise! It's terribly costly.

Good Leadership

Joshua doesn't want compromise in their future. The mark of a good leader isn't what happens when he is there but when he is gone.

A little boy was trying to lead a very large dog. He said, "I'm waiting to see which way he wants to go and then I'm going to take him there."

I don't know about you but I'm up to my ears with leaders who want to take a vote on the truth. Leaders who put their finger in the wind to see which way it's blowing and then go that way. It's not that a leader is to steam-roller ideas through – a leader is a servant to the people. But leaders must lead. Leaders must lead away from the grey to the black and white – no compromise over what matters most.

Joshua feared most that there would be no difference between his people and the nations around them. There is a sense in which we ought to have convictions and be different.

Would you be surprised if you caught me cheating or in a lie? You should be! We should be able to tell who are those people who do not sell-out. Don't expect God's blessing if we settle for comfortable Christianity.

A pastor named Tim Keller says that, *"Sin isn't just doing bad things. Sin is also making good things into ultimate things. Sin is building your life and meaning on anything, even a good thing, more than on God."*

Marriage is a good thing, but if we focus our identity on our husband or wife, over time we will become possessive and jealous. Money is a useful tool, but if we focus our life on it, we'll be stressed out about losing it. If we focus our life on a good cause, even a Christian cause, and we're focused more there than on Jesus, we can become judgmental and proud. When we focus on anything other than relationship with Jesus and His kingdom, our world shrinks down to the size of me and mine. It's not just Christians that do this. This is a human problem.

Joshua is saying, be different! "Not one of the good promises the Lord your God gave you has failed. Every promise has been fulfilled." God also promised that if they drifted they would be removed from the land until they learned their lesson. God doesn't give up on His children but He will discipline them.

Last Words

Remember that we are looking at some of the last words of Joshua. I came across some interesting last words of other people.

Lord Palmerstone said, *"Die, my dear doctor? That is the last thing I shall do."* Oscar Wilde said: *"Either this wallpaper goes or I do."*

Do you know what Joshua is busy saying? God's way is better than ours. We will be the loser when we compromise. Disobedience is costly.

I like the words of a lawyer: *"The Christian has a far greater future than he has a past."* That's a good thing to remember. We rarely get that kind of truth from the young. An old man like Joshua can tell us some important things before he died.

Whatever our age, we all need to hear what Joshua communicates. We must know what it is to obey and to have a personal faith and personal responsibility to His Word. Any person or anything that influences us away from our relationship with God today is a danger to our life. Love the Lord our God. His cause really is worthy. A cause worth dying for.

(10) HALLOWED

There's an old story about a boy praying and saying: Our Father who art in heaven HAROLD be your name."

Once we know who we are talking to in prayer, the first thing Jesus gets into is HALLOWED be your name. What does that mean? The word HALLOWED is rarely used in general English.

But it's a great idea to HALLOW His name. To treat it as sacred. To HALLOW means to make something our ultimate concern. The most important, the most crucial, the most sacred – the supreme aim. That is to HALLOW something. And Jesus says, "This comes FIRST in all prayer."

I want to show you that life should be about this. To understand the world and our place in it we have to pray and adore God. Praise and adoration is really what life's all about.

We need to know about the **PRETENCE OF PRAISE.**
We need to understand the **PRIORITY OF PRAISE.**
We need what I call the **PENDULUM OF PRAISE.**

1) PRETENCE OF PRAISE.

Jesus starts by calling our attention to pretence in praise, "When you pray don't be like the hypocrites." Right off we think, He's meaning people living double lives. I think Jesus is talking about hypocritical prayers.

Hypocrisy
A hypocrite is somebody who is not consistent. There's a kind of person who prays in the open but not in secret. Why? Because they want to be seen as spiritual people. And therefore they only pray when they're getting what they really want. In secret they get no acclaim for prayer, and therefore they don't pray. There's a kind of person who only prays when their ultimate concern is at stake.

The way you can tell true prayer is when what you most want is God. Just to adore and enjoy Him. He is the supreme thing in your life. If that's true we'll pray all the time. If we only pray when we're in trouble, or when things get bad – when things get better we'll stop praying. What's going on? What we're really doing in secret tells us who our God is.

The Solitude Test

William Temple tell us that our religion is what we do with our solitude. That's what Jesus is saying. The way to find out our ultimate concern, that thing that really makes our life go is to see what we do in secret. When we're alone. When there's nothing that we have to do. What do we think about?

Do we think about owning a better house? Do we dream of a better car? Falling in love? Business success? Professional acclaim? Achievement? Our hobbies? Our comfort? What do we think about when we don't have to think about anything else? What do we do with our secrecy? Jesus says, "That's what you adore the most."

If the thing we adore is not God, we only pray when that thing is in jeopardy, when that thing is at stake. Therefore, we'll have an inconsistent prayer life. We'll pray sometimes, like when we're in trouble. We only pray when the family is in need. Our finances are crashing.

We always pray when our greatest treasure is at stake. The consistency of our prayer life will tell who our God is. That's why we talk about the PRETENCE OF PRAYER.

Everybody praises. Everybody spends their secrecy praising. But if it's not God, we'll only pray sometimes when things are at stake. I'm convicted by this. Jesus is saying: "The most unmistakable way to tell that your Christianity is real, that it's not just a matter of external forces, that you've been touched by God, is if you pray consistently in secret. And do you praise God in secret?"

Do we spend lots of time consistently praying and enjoying God? Here's why! People see us coming to church. They see our moral behaviour. There are all kinds of other external and even selfish rewards for almost every other part of Christianity.

I know there are people who come into Christianity because they just want to be included in a supportive group. I know that some people get involved because they love to feel that they've got the truth.

I know some people are emotionally needy and need something. And they never go deeper and ask, 'Is this true?' They never really give their heart over. They never really meet God. As a result they come in and seem very active – but it's all on the basis of externals.

They need a supportive group. They need something to cling to. They like feeling "I'm on the inside." They'll be there for a while. Then they'll suddenly leave. Something will come up in their life and their Christianity will all fall apart. Why? It was all externals.

The Deception Test
How do we know we're not deceiving ourselves and into pretence? Here it is – what we are in secret! What do we do with our solitude? Do we pray regularly? Do we love to praise? Do we adore God? Is this the thing that keeps us going? Or, do we spend our secrecy day-dreaming about things that are obviously more important to us than God?

Then our religion is a matter of the externals. We really don't have that power that Jesus talked about. It comes to those who make adoration of God the *priority* of our life.

There's PRETENCE – We give the impression of praise but it's superficial, not what we really are. Praise is a priority.

2) THE PRIORITY OF PRAISE.

It's absolutely essential we have a full and flourishing praise life. Praise is vital. "Hallowed be Your name" comes before what? "give us this day our daily bread and forgive us our debts." We get into praising before asking. That's petitionary: "Give to me because I have all these needs."

Praise First
Go to praise before you go to petition. Not only that – go to praise before you go to confession, "forgive us." It's not just first by accident. It's not just a set of steps to God – start with praise and then go to confession and asking. It's first because praise is supposed to frame the others. Praise is the context for the others. Praise is to dominate and saturate the others. Praise is to dominate not just prayer but all of life. Why?

Because petition means how we look at the world. Confession is how we look at ourselves. Jesus tells us that all the problems we have in relating to the world or ourselves are really problems of adoration. If we don't hallow God. If we hallow anything more than God, the problems will show up in petition and confession.

When we do *petition* we're saying, "I've got needs." When we do *confession* we're saying, "I've got problems." The issues in both of those areas are really problems of adoration. People say, "I did wrong and I asked forgiveness and I know God gave it to me but I can't forgive myself." My question is this: what do you do with your secret time? What do you hallow the most? What is it you adore the most? Is it success? Is it sex appeal? Is it comfort or the approval of other people? Is it love of life or love of family?

Most Hallowed?

What is it that you most hallow? That will completely control your view of yourself. And confession will be completely driven by that. You'll only feel you've failed if you've failed one of these things. What we hallow impacts us. If we hallow anything other than God it will distort our view of ourselves. It will distort confession so that it's all filled with guilt and frustration.

When someone says, "I can't forgive myself." What they mean is this: "I hallow something more than God and it won't forgive me. I know God forgives me but it won't forgive me."

A man had been unfaithful to his wife. She had forgiven him and received him back. The people around him forgave. But he said, "I can't forgive myself." He came from a strict family where sexual sin was worse than any other kind. And even though his parents were dead he felt he had disappointed them. "I can't forgive myself." His problem was in the area of self-image – yes! He needs to forgive himself – yes! But his problem is prior. He needed to demote his parents. He needed to get them out of the holy place in his life. He needed to get them off the throne. The grace of God wasn't driving him. What he got his self-image from was that he lived up to his parents' expectations. He failed, so he said, "I can't forgive myself." Sounds humble? No – it's a failure of adoration. It's a misuse of our solitude. We're not hallowing!

Adoration

Everything comes from adoration. If we can say, "Hallowed be your Name," we have no problem saying, "forgive us our debts." We've got to do *adoration* before we get to *confession*. But we also must do *adoration* before getting to *petition*. We can ask: "Give us this day our daily bread." What is bread? It's the basic we've got to have. It's doesn't say, 'Our daily dessert, apple pie or cappuccino." It's *bread*!

Praying and Making Matters Worse!

I've talked to people who say, "I've prayed but I get no peace. I don't think God is interested in me." Here's why. What if we go to God and say, "I've got to get this promotion or my life is over. It's bread! I've got to have it." No wonder we lack peace. Why? If we're hallowing our career – whatever we hallow is the thing running our life. If we ever think about losing it we go to pieces.

The reason we pray about anxiety but are still eaten up by it is this. It's a failure of adoration. We have to demote our job. We've got to get it out of the hallowed place. Don't you see, praise and adoration of God is the thing that will heal our view of the world and our view of ourselves. It must dominate. We must be great at it. Adoration is looking at God and saying, 'Amazing, everything is coming back into focus."

A pastor talks of preaching through the Lord's Prayer. He had heard or read somewhere that adoration has to come before asking. "Don't come to God with gimme-type prayers," he says, "I believed it but never really understood it." A week later he was visiting with an elderly lady who said that her whole life had been changed by this common-sense. Spending time on adoration gave her a truer perspective. She said, "By the time I get to my prayer requests instead of being so worried, I lay them in His hands once and just relax." He said, "The teacher was taught."

The Key

This is the key. All our failures are failures of *adoration*. We have to get our life back into perspective.

Can you imagine a father taking his young child into a great toy shop and saying, "Look at these toys, do you like them? You'll not have one. I'm going to spend all my life keeping you miserable." What would happen to that child? The child would have a distorted view of life and him or herself. If they can't trust their father how can they trust anything?

The Bible tells us that way back at the beginning of time God put two people into a garden and said there is only one tree you are not to eat from, enjoy all the rest. Why say that? He wanted them to love and trust Him. But they were deceived. They believed the lie that God was keeping the best from them and this proves it. God has not got your best interests at heart. You can't trust Him.

That lie slips into our hearts. And our entire view of the world and ourselves is distorted because we think God is like that father at the shop. If we can't praise God we won't be able to praise anything else. If we can't trust God we won't be able to trust anything. If we can praise God we can't start praising anything. If we can trust God we won't trust others.

We're not stupid and naive. But we're able to say: 'Look how great this is.' If we can't praise God we're likely to say, "Look how awful this is. It started out good but it will probably end up bad."

Healed Through Adoration

Adoration heals us. We see that because God won't give us everything and He won't give us nothing. It's intrinsic in children. Even if they have nice parents, if you cross their will, "We can't go the circus, we don't have the time." "I want to go." "We can't but we can play that game you like." "No! I don't want to do it." Because you wouldn't give everything I want it proves to me you don't want me to have anything. Where does a child get that? I'm not talking about neglectful parents but good parents. It's intrinsic in our hearts. We have a basic ingratitude. Adoration is the only thing that heals us of that.

Self-Hatred

That's the reason you hate yourself. Or, deny your sinfulness. Adoration enables us to see who we are and yet accept it. Adoration enables us to see the world as it is and yet trust. Without it we're totally distorted. Adoration heals the heart.

One last thing and it's most important. How do we adore? Jesus Christ gives us a little practical key. I call it the *pendulum* of praise.

3) THE PENDULUM OF PRAISE

The basic way to praise is a pendulum. We pray to our *Father*. This means we look at how loving He is. We can look at the depth of His love

and the width of His mercy and the amazing grace that comes down freely from Him to us His children.
We also pray to our Father who is in *heaven*. He is majestic. He is powerful. He is above us. It's only as those two things come together does it work.

Pendulums are funny. The further they go to one side the further they go to the other side. The beauty of adoration is this. The more we see His love, the more we see His greatness and glory. It's set into relief. The more we see His greatness the more we see what His love means to us.

When I think about being a father, I long for my children to be successful and happy. I think that God must feel like that too as a Father. The difference is, He is a HEAVENLY FATHER and He has the power to make dreams come true. Knowing He is a FATHER is re-assuring. But knowing He is a HEAVENLY Father is liberating! He will only give us right and good things at the right and proper time.

A woman said, "I have a relationship with God but it has nothing to do with Jesus." She was asked, "Do you believe God forgives you." "Yes I do." So she was asked, "What does it cost Him to forgive you?" She said, "I can't believe that He would send anyone to hell." "Okay, you won't say God is a holy God, that He is perfect and will not abide evil forever. You won't say that He is too good to allow evil to be permanent but will deal with it. But that He is also merciful in taking its penalty upon Himself and dealing with it."

If you only go so far, what does it cost your God to forgive you? Nothing! If we don't believe in hell we have no idea of a God who would take hell into His own heart. A God who would suffer and die and pour His wrath out on His Son that we may be saved.

The more holy we see Him to be the more loving we see Him to be. The more loving we see Him to be the more holy we see Him to be. That's why Jesus Christ said, "No-one knows the Father except the Son and those to whom the Son reveals Him."

Objections
People say, "That's narrow-minded." That doesn't mean we can't be wise without Jesus. It doesn't mean we can't be moral. But we won't know the

Father as He is. Only on the Cross do we have a totally holy God and a loving God.

That lady said, “God doesn’t expect us to be perfect.” If so, what does it cost Him to forgive? Not much! Unless we have a God who came to earth and dies for us on the Cross in order to save us – we don’t understand Him and appreciate.

Clear Sighted
We can’t have a totally holy and loving God unless we come to Him through Jesus. Adoration is a pendulum. The further it comes to this side the further it goes to the other side.

He is a Father and He is a Heavenly Father. He is Heavenly but He is a Father. It heats us up. It creates adoration. It will melt away the distortions in our view of ourselves and the world.

‘All praise we would render
O help us to see
Tis only the splendour
Of light hideth Thee.’

Prayer
Our Father in Heaven,
Teach us to hallow Your Name.
It’s healthy and healing.
Only as we do so will we see the Son for Who He is.

Copyright
Good News Broadcasting Association (GB)
Ranskill DN22 8NN England
Email: info@gnba.net
Web site: www.gnba.net